Catholicism
Today

Matthew F. Kohmescher, S.M.

PAULIST PRESS
New York / Ramsey

Nihil Obstat
Reverend John J. Jennings
Censor Deputatus

Imprimatur
Daniel E. Pilarczyk, V.G.
Auxiliary Bishop of Cincinnati

June 27, 1980

The *nihil obstat* and *imprimatur* are official declarations that a book or
pamphlet is free of doctrinal or moral error. No implication is contained
therein that those who have granted the *nihil obstat* and *imprimatur* agree
with the contents, opinions or statements expressed.

ISBN: 0-8091-2335-5

Library of Congress
Catalog Card Number: 80-82085

Published by Paulist Press
Editorial Office: 1865 Broadway, New York, N.Y. 10023
Business Office: 545 Island Road, Ramsey, N.J. 07446

Printed and bound in the
United States of America

CONTENTS

INTRODUCTION

Like Topsy in *Uncle Tom's Cabin* this book just seemed to grow. While teaching a very basic course on the Catholic Church today, I struggled to discover a good text for student use. Not finding one to fit my own purpose, I began to assemble my own lecture notes for duplication. What appears here is a result of all my own reading, discussion, and reflection. When this process is repeated a number of times with different colleagues and students involved, it is difficult to recognize what comes from where. Whenever possible I have endeavored to give credit for specific points and insights. For what is common knowledge or the product of discussion with colleagues and students, no formal acknowledgment is made.

At the end of each chapter I have listed just a few of the many books and articles that I found helpful. Many more could be mentioned and still others will be available as this book comes to print. In addition, I strongly recommend the *New Catholic Encyclopedia* which contains an almost unbelievable wealth of material on all topics covered here; I do wish to acknowledge my own indebtedness to it. Further, much good reading is to be found in current Catholic periodicals and newspapers, both diocesan and national.

I would like to thank all those who have helped in the growth and development of this publication. There are my colleagues: Dr. Mary Durkin and Fr. Mark Paduk who used a preliminary version of this book in their classes, Ms. Darlene Tempelton who assisted in the final composition, especially of Chapters 1 and 23, and Fr. James Heft, S.M. who helped re-write the chapter on infallibility. Next come the unsung he-roes, the typists, who performed yeoman service as this book went through several revisions: Tina Blanda, Lynda Crane, Leslie Harrison, and Suzanne Ksycewski. Finally, I must give sincere credit to my students whose questions, comments and criticisms have helped this book grow from a few dittoed sheets to what it is today. Many of the discussion questions were suggested by them.

While giving credit where credit is due, I must assume fi-nal responsibility for what follows. I have endeavored to pre-sent a simple and balanced picture of where the Catholic Church is today without going into great depth on any one point. Like the Church, this book too is a pilgrim that will continue to grow and develop as we move through the 1980's.

1 THE CHURCH THROUGH THE AGES

If we go back in time and take an overall look at the history of the Catholic Church, we should attain a greater understanding of the changes that are currently taking place and a greater insight into why the Church is making them. It is hoped that by becoming better acquainted with the history of our faith community, we shall become more fully aware of the problems of today and see in a limited way what must be done for the future.

In studying Church history, there are four main ideas that are helpful in arriving at a good overall view of the Church throughout the twenty centuries of its existence. They are:

• The Church has evolved.
• Each cultural epoch had its impact.
• Each age of the Church had its problems.
• The Church today is still alive—growing, evolving, developing.

Before considering these four key points, let us first look over the following time line. It should give us a fairly good idea of the chronology of Church history and where these important events fit into the history of the world as a whole.

Church History		World History
The Christ event: Jesus' death, resurrection and ascension	29	Tiberius Roman Emperor
Council of Jerusalem; Gentiles are admitted into the Christian faith without first having to become Jews	50	
First persecution; Sts. Peter and Paul martyred	65	Rome burns; Nero emperor
Edict of Milan establishes religious freedom	313	Constantine emperor
Council of Nicaea defines personhood of Christ; Nicene Creed	325	
	410	Alaric, leader of the Visigoths, captures Rome; beginning of the so-called "Dark Ages"
Benedictine monastic rule written; rise of monasticism in the West	530	
	622	Foundation of Islam by Mohammed
	721	Battle of Tours prevents Moslem incursion into France
Donation of Pepin establishes Papal States	756	
Charlemagne crowned Holy Roman Emperor by Pope Leo III	800	
	850–1000	Viking invasions of Europe
Western (Roman) and Eastern (Orthodox) churches split	1054	
	1066	William the Conqueror invades England
Beginning of Church/State conflict when Pope Gregory VII excommunicates Henry IV for consecrating bishops	1077	
First Crusade called by Pope Urban II	1095	
Church/state conflict accelerates with the murder of Archbishop Thomas Becket	1170	
Dominican and Franciscan orders established	1209–1217	

Church History		World History
IV Lateran Council; annual confession and Communion	1215	Magna Carta
"Babylonian Captivity"; Pope lives in Avignon, France	1304–1377	
Great Schism; two popes one in Rome, one in Avignon	1378–1417	
Spain reconquered from the Moslems	1492	New World discovered
Martin Luther posts his ninety-five Theses; Reformation begins	1517	St. Peter's in Rome being rebuilt; Michelangelo main architect
First Catholic missionaries arrive in Mexico	1526	Cortez
Henry VIII of England breaks from the Roman Catholic Church; Anglican Church established	1534	
Calvin establishes first Reformed Church in Geneva	1536	
Jesuits founded by St. Ignatius Loyola to combat Protestantism	1544	
Council of Trent	1545–1563	
	1594	St. Augustine, Florida founded
	1607	Jamestown
Colony of Maryland founded as a haven for persecuted Catholics	1634	
Fr. Junipero Serra founds first mission in California	1769	
	1775	American Revolution begins
	1789	French Revolution begins
	1848	Communist Manifesto written
Immaculate Conception defined	1854	
Vatican I: papal infallibility	1869–1870	
	1914–1918	World War I
	1939–1945	World War II
Assumption of Mary defined	1950	
Vatican II	1962–1965	
First non-Italian Pope in 400 years elected	1978	

THE CHURCH HAS EVOLVED

Organization

If we could be miraculously transported in time back to the days of the earliest Church, what type of organization would we find? It would probably seem strange to someone from the twentieth-century institution-oriented Catholic Church to see how little organization there was immediately after the ascension of Jesus. To begin with, there were no church buildings; there were no priests, deacons, or sisters; there was no Bible as we know it today. There were only a handful of dedicated men and women who had experienced Christ during his life on earth and who now wanted to tell the whole world about their experience.

The first Church leaders were the twelve apostles, but they soon found that as the infant Church grew, they needed to spend so much of their time ministering to the temporal needs of the people that they had little time left to spread the news of the Gospel. Therefore they chose men and women to assist them. By the end of the first century these deacons and deaconesses did much of the practical work in the Church— preparing people for baptism, taking the Eucharist to the sick, distributing clothing and food to the poor so that the apostles and, later, the bishops could be freed to teach and to conduct the eucharistic celebration.

The exact origin of the role of priest/bishop is rather vague. It appears that some early Church communities grew around an "ordained" leader, but other communities (e.g., Corinth) did not. By the year 160 the system of priests and bishops had been organized in a way similar to the organization of today. The congregation elected the bishop (remember, churches were much smaller then than they are now) and there are instances of charismatic men who were not yet even baptized being elected to bishoprics. St. Ambrose of Milan (c. 350) is a good example of this.

The earliest clergy lived a life little different from that of their fellow Christians. Many were married, with families, and earned their living primarily at some trade or profession. Gradually, however, as the Church communities grew larger and more responsibility began to fall on the priesthood, it became the custom for them to be supported totally by the Church community. Thus by the fourth century most priests were engaged only in religious work.

With the breakdown of Roman civil authority and the repeated barbarian invasions of the Empire, the role of the bishop as a civil as well as a spiritual authority grew. During this time, people began turning to the bishop of Rome as the supreme authority. Reasons for this were varied. People were used to looking to Rome as the seat of civil authority; Rome was central and largely untouched by the waves of barbarian invasions that disrupted the northern dioceses; Rome had a long tradition as a Christian city and was the site of the martyrdom of the two primary apostles, Peter and Paul. Pope Leo I (440–461) was the first Pope who we know claimed universal authority, and although not everyone accepted the idea at the time, it steadily grew until in 1075 Pope Gregory could declare that all Christians were obligated to obey him and that those who did not could be eternally damned. He even reserved to himself the right to punish and depose monarchs who disagreed with him.

Undoubtedly, the most important man in medieval Europe was the Pope. As a secular ruler he had direct authority over much of Italy; as Supreme Pontiff he used the threat of interdict and excommunication to bring recalcitrant monarchs into line. It is true that some of the medieval popes used this power to further their own personal goals and that there were abuses of the sacred office. It also must be remembered that the medieval mentality and moral climate were much different from ours today and that many people were not much disturbed by a Pope who was a military leader or even by one who had a mistress and illegitimate children.

It is safe to say that without the Catholic bishops, medieval secular governments would not have functioned as effectively as they did. Most bishops came from the ranks of the nobility. Usually they were an extremely well-educated group, many of them having taken advantage of a university education. Often, at least during the early Middle Ages, the bishops would be the only men at court who could read and write. Because of this they often held important government posts. This led to an inevitable conflict between religious and secular duties.

The duties of a priest during the Middle Ages were much the same as they are today: saying daily Mass, hearing confessions, baptizing, teaching and preaching, burying the dead. Most parish priests came from the lower classes; often a lord would choose one of the more intelligent young men on his land and pay for his schooling. When the youth felt himself ready for ordination, he presented himself to the bishop and took a three-day exam on the Catholic faith. If he passed, he was ordained.

The Protestant Reformation severely curtailed the political power of the Popes as entire countries, now Protestant, refused to recognize the authority of the papacy. The Council of Trent, reacting against some of the evils that had caused the Reformation, looked at the abuses in the Church hierarchy and attempted to correct them. Popes and bishops became less and less political figures and more and more spiritual ones. Seminaries were established throughout Europe to insure that the young men who became priests received proper education. Reacting against their excessive involvement in the secular world prior to Trent, priests moved further and further away from secular involvement. Unfortunately, they tended to move to the opposite extreme, and social intercourse with the secular world ceased almost entirely.

Vatican II caused the Church to take another close look at itself, and various changes resulted. Many bishops wanted the Church to be somewhat more democratic, so now there is more emphasis on collegiality. Since the Church is concerned with the "whole" person in the "whole" world, its priestly ministers need to be formed accordingly. Thus, young men are now encouraged to enter the seminary only after they have completed college, rather than before high school. Their formation may include graduate classes taken on a college campus, and will encompass a period of special internship in the priestly ministry. Further, most priests now mingle freely with lay people, and some have been involved in non-traditional work such as politics.

Teaching

After Jesus' resurrection, his followers were concerned not with writing down what had happened while Christ was here on earth but with preaching the Jesus experience to all peoples of the world. The disciples fully expected Jesus to return soon and to establish the kingdom of heaven. However, about thirty years passed and Jesus still had not returned. The infant Church was being sporadically persecuted throughout the Roman Empire, and those who had personally known Jesus were either being martyred or dying of old age. Christians suddenly realized that there was a danger of losing all the knowledge possessed by those persons who had actually known Jesus. The different traditions about Jesus needed to be written down. Thus came the Gospels, which were composed in their current form between the years 60 and 120.

After the legalization of Christianity (313), churchmen found themselves with the leisure to begin debating seriously various theological questions. The most important issue was the nature of Christ—the extent to which Jesus was either human or divine. Debates on this and other questions were heated, and several ecumenical councils were called to deal with the problem. In addition to the various decrees of the councils, creeds were written in an attempt to define exactly what it is that we, as Christians, believe. One of the most important of these creeds the bishops composed for the most part at the Council of Nicaea in 325. This is the creed which we still say at Mass today.

The early Middle Ages (400–1000) was a period of intense missionary activity in the Christian Church. As barbarian tribes overran the Roman fortresses in Gaul and Asia Minor, Christian missionaries went out to proclaim the Gospel. Foremost in the rank of these were the Irish monks (Ireland had been converted by St. Patrick in the fifth century) who were largely responsible for bringing Christianity to Scotland and most of northern Europe. By the year 1000, most of Europe had been converted to Christianity.

During the reign of the Franco-German king Charlemagne, his chancellor, Alcuin, realized that the only way to obtain educated young men for the priesthood would be for the Church to open schools. Thus, Alcuin began what came to be known as cathedral schools. These schools taught basic reading, math, theology, music and Latin. During the early Middle Ages the only persons who bothered to get an education were the clergy, and conversely, if a young man wanted to be educated, the only way to do it was to enter the clergy.

Sometime in the twelfth century the first universities were founded. As the constant threat of barbarian invasions decreased, young men found that they had both the time and inclination to pursue their education. Medieval universities taught only three subjects: theology, law (canon and civil), and medicine. At first all university students were religious; it was not until the fourteenth and fifteenth centuries that laymen began to enter the universities. When they did, they were usually the sons of noblemen or, in England, the sons of the rising middle class.

The universities offered a climate for abstract theological and philosophical thought, thus giving rise to a group of scholars known today as Scholastics. Pre-eminent among these men was St. Thomas Aquinas. Aquinas synthesized the work of the great ancient philosophers, especially Aristotle, and merged it with contemporary Christian reflection to form a school of thought known as Thomism. Using this system as his base, he went on to write his great masterpiece, the *Summa Theologica* (1266–74) which summarizes and treats every aspect of Christian belief. After the Council of Trent the *Summa Theologica* formed the basis of most philosophy and theology courses taught in Catholic universities and seminaries until the 1960's.

During the Protestant Reformation, both the Reformers and the Catholics realized that they needed a fairly simple way of presenting religious truths to the people. Martin Luther first conceived the simple question and answer format known as the catechism. Roman Catholics noted its effectiveness and adapted it for their own use.

Today there are a variety of ways in which we present religious truths to the faithful. It has been said by some that we live in a post-literate society which no longer relies primarily on the printed word for education. Our presentation of the faith takes this into account. Not only do we teach from catechisms and other texts, but we also use a multitude of audiovisual materials. We are a pluralistic society, using many different ways to teach the one, eternal truth of Jesus Christ.

Worship

The worship service of the Catholic Church has its roots in the worship services of the Jewish people. The first Christians were Jews, and as such they worshiped in the Jewish synagogue. The synagogue service consisted of a series of readings from the Old Testament, chanted psalms, prayers and a sermon. When this service was over, the Christians would gather together and celebrate a very simple Eucharist. After the first century, when the Church became mostly Gentile, Christians added a word service, very similar to the Jewish synagogue service, to the Eucharist, giving us the Mass in basically the same form that we celebrate it today.

In the early Church everyone participated in the liturgy. The priest/bishop stood at a table-like altar, facing his congregation. There was a strong community spirit, because everyone knew everyone else. Knowing your fellow worshiper had great importance during the years of persecution. Rarely did you allow someone who was not well known to attend the liturgy, for fear that he might betray the congregation to the Roman authorities.

After the legalization of the Church in 313, the worship service began to change. Priests received the respect that one would give a Roman senator or any other person of high rank; part of that respect was to be allowed to wear distinctive clothing and to have candles and emblems carried before them. The Mass itself became a solemn ritual. During the centuries between 400 and 1100, the altar began to be moved away from its central position amid the congregation until it faced the back wall and the priest had to celebrate Mass with his back to the congregation. The eucharistic prayer began to be said silently. The responses of the people were either dropped or were sung by a trained choir. Reception of the Eucharist ceased to be the focal point of the Mass; it was replaced by the elevation of the consecrated host. There were instances during the Middle Ages when people would ask the priest to raise the host higher or keep it elevated longer.

For the average medieval man, God was an unreachable figure. God was awesome, grand, far away, unconcerned with the problems of a lowly serf or peasant. Because the people could not read, they were unfamiliar with the Bible and stories about Jesus, so Jesus too became an awe-inspiring figure. God and Jesus were totally beyond the comprehension of most medieval persons. This led to the rise of the cult of saints. A saint had lived on earth and had known all the problems and temptations that all humans know. Because the saints had lived a normal human life, the people felt closer to them than to a God who was far away and possibly unconcerned with the many problems of day-to-day living. And so, people prayed to their saints, asking them to intercede with God.

Over the centuries, many abuses had crept into Catholic worship. The Council of Trent attempted to correct many of these. Missals were standardized, so that all priests everywhere said and did the same thing when celebrating the Mass. However, the Mass remained in Latin and it remained silent. Many Catholics prayed their private devotions during Mass. The worship of the people would change very little in the four hundred years between Trent and Vatican II.

In the past fifty years the Mass has changed from a time for private devotions to the action of a community worshiping God together. Due to a series of reforms begun before Vatican II, we now have Mass in the vernacular with the prayers said aloud and the people responding. The main thrust of many of the reforms has been to bring the Mass back to where we were in the early Church: a community of believers worshiping God together.

CULTURAL IMPACT AND PROBLEMS CREATED

Christianity came forth out of Judaism and was deeply influenced by it. Jesus himself was a Jew, not a Christian, and all of his first followers were Jews. Therefore, they interpreted their new faith in Jesus in the light of their Jewish beliefs and customs. However, Jesus had told his disciples: "Go out into all the world and baptize." This meant going out to the non-

Jewish people, the Gentiles, and it is from this going out that the infant Church began to have its first problems.

Many of the early followers of Jesus, including the disciples, felt that if Gentiles wanted to be baptized as Christians, they must first become Jews. However, the Gentiles, while eager to become Christians, were not eager to take on all the obligations imposed by Judaism. The ensuing debate led to the calling of the first Christian council, called the Council of Jerusalem, about the year 50. At this council the twelve apostles met with St. Paul and other apostles to the Gentiles and decided that, while Gentile converts did not have to become Jews, they had an obligation to obey certain Jewish laws.

	CULTURE	
	Impact on Church Life and Expressions	Creates New Challenges
JUDAISM	Liturgy, Scripture	Gentile Converts
FEUDALISM	Organization, Feast Days, Cult of Saints	Church-State Relations, Simony, Lay Investiture
TODAY	Reform of Liturgy, Ecumenism, Collegiallity	Women Priests, Intercommunion Divorce and Remarriage

The influx of so many Gentile converts would cause many of Christianity's problems in the next two hundred years. As long as the new religion remained predominantly a sect of Judaism, it was protected from persecution. The Roman Empire required that all persons worship the Roman emperors, not necessarily because they actually believed the emperor to be divine, but as a way of pledging allegiance to the Roman state. The Jewish people, because of their long history of worshiping only one God, were exempted from this requirement. So were the early Christians. But as Christianity began to sever its ties with Judaism and was no longer seen as a Jewish sect, it became subject to regulation by Roman authorities. However, the Christians refused to worship the emperor. Therefore, Christianity was declared illegal and subversive, and the persecutions began.

The Empire intermittently persecuted the Church for about two hundred and fifty years. Most of the time Christians were left alone to worship as they pleased, but occasionally a major persecution would be ordered and hundreds of Christians would die for their faith. A person accused of being a Christian was brought before the Roman magistrate and asked to burn incense before a statue of the emperor and to revile Christ. Most Christians refused. However, some people, when faced with the prospect of torture and death, denied their faith. These persons, called apostates, often later regretted their actions and asked to be forgiven and received again into the Church. At first the Church was reluctant to readmit them, but later it set up a system whereby, after completing several years of strict penance, the apostate could again be admitted to the Eucharist.

In 313 Emperor Constantine legalized Christianity, and within fifty years the once persecuted faith became the religion of the Roman Empire. Because of this the Church was free to grow, to develop, and to reflect upon itself and its teachings. But just as, during any period of growth, problems are apt to arise, so it was with the young Church. The first of these problems came when theologians began to try to understand exactly who Christ was. Was he God? Man? Both? Several early councils were called to deal with this question: Nicaea (325), Constantinople (381), Ephesus (431), and Chalcedon (451).

Our belief today, that Jesus Christ had two complete natures in one divine personality comes from these councils. Unfortunately, this explanation did not satisfy everyone, and throughout the early Middle Ages various heresies arose saying that Christ was either completely divine or completely human. Arianism, perhaps the most important of these heresies, believed that Jesus was inferior to God the Father. Between the years 320 and 500, Arianism was a problem with which the Church had to contend. At one time, most of the people of northern Greece, northern Europe and Spain were Arians.

Almost as soon as Christianity was legalized in 313, the Roman Emperor began to want to have a say in directing Church policies. It is interesting to note that the first ecumenical council, the Council of Nicaea, was not called by the Pope or the bishops, but by Emperor Constantine. The emperor felt that, because most of his subjects were Christian, and because he had to keep peace in the Empire, one of the best ways to do it would be to have a voice in Church affairs. This tendency of rulers to interfere in the directing of the Church would persist strongly throughout the Middle Ages and is still present in some countries today.

The Middle Ages

The Church/state conflict would be an especially important problem during the Middle Ages. Medieval kings felt that they should be the ones to appoint the bishops for the dioceses in their countries. They wanted bishops who knew the areas in which they worked, not foreigners appointed by the Pope. This led to several conflicts between various rulers and the Popes, and there are a few cases where a bishop, who felt that his primary loyalty was to Rome, was either exiled or assassinated by the henchmen of a disappointed king. The problem was partially solved at the Concordat of Worms in 1122 when it was decided that bishops would be elected by the clergy in the presence of the king to whom they were required to do homage.

The Middle Ages have been termed rather romantically as the Age of Faith. Religion was an extremely important thing to most medieval people. For the poor (about 95% of the population) it was the only consolation they had in their short and dreary lives. They looked forward to going to Mass, and they especially looked forward to the many feast days. The concept of a five-day work week is very modern; during the Middle Ages the only days on which the poor did not have to work were the feast days of the saints. Because of this, the Church saw that there were many feast days in the year, thus giving the poor some relief from the drudgery of their daily lives. The Church also regulated the lives of the nobility. The primary job of the medieval knight was to fight. He was seldom happy doing anything else. The Church knew this, and thus it made laws which tried to regulate where and how often a knight fought. Concepts such as the Peace of God and Truce of God were instituted to regulate warfare. Mostly these benefited the innocent civilians who often were the ones harmed by battles taking place in their villages and fields. The Peace of God outlawed war against women, clergy and other non-combatants; the Truce of God disallowed war on holy days or during Lent and Advent.

It was partly in order to regulate the constant internal fighting of the medieval knight that Pope Urban II came up with the idea of a Crusade. The Crusades were a series of battles fought both in the Holy Land and in Spain to free the once Christian lands from Moslem domination. The Pope called the first Crusade in 1095 against the Saracens in Palestine. The Crusades continued intermittently until 1492, when the last of the Moslems were driven out of Spain. Generally the Crusades were unsuccessful (they did not reconquer the Holy Land); however, they did give the knights a place to fight and a reason to fight, and economically they were of great benefit to Europe.

Two great schisms took place during the later years of the Middle Ages. The first of these was the final and complete break between the Church of western Europe and the eastern Church (Greece, Asia Minor, and Russia). Although both Churches believed in the same Christ, the cultural differences between East and West had become too great to be bridged. In 1054 the final split between these two branches of the Christian Church came when the Pope in Rome and the Patriarch in Constantinople excommunicated one another.

The second schism, known in history as the Great Schism, began in 1378. Prior to this, in 1305, the Pope had moved from Rome to a French city named Avignon in order to escape the constant political turmoil in Rome. Avignon belonged to the papacy, and it was a peaceful place from which the Pope could pursue his duties. However, many people wanted the papacy returned to Rome. In 1377 Pope Gregory XI did return, only to die the next year. Immediately the cardinals came together to elect a new Pope. Unfortunately, the new Pope soon made himself very unpopular with the non-Italian cardinals, many of whom returned to France and elected a non-Italian Pope. So now the Church had two Popes—one in Rome and one in Avignon. Europe was divided about which Pope to support. The Holy Roman Empire, England, the Netherlands, Castile, Hungary, Poland and Portugal supported Rome, while France, Scotland, Luxembourg and Austria supported Avignon. This sorry state of affairs lasted until 1417 when at the Council of Constance Europe was again united under one Pope.

The Reformation

It would be an oversimplification to say that the Catholic Church of the fourteenth and fifteenth centuries was corrupt.

However it did have very many problems. Church offices were regularly being sold to the highest bidder; many bishops had two or three dioceses, sometimes in different countries; many popes and bishops were more interested in secular affairs than in the affairs of the Church; the different religious orders had become lax. In order to bring some of these evils to the attention of the people, an Augustinian monk named Martin Luther nailed a list of ninety-five theses on the door of the Wittenburg Cathedral. Martin Luther did not intend to challenge the Church; he did intend to initiate a debate among other members of the clergy and university professors. But things snowballed. Due partly to the political climate of the times, Luther soon found himself the head of a reforming group that within the next twenty years would break all ties with the Roman Catholic Church. Other reformers, in other countries, would follow his example until, by 1600, England, Scotland, Switzerland, Sweden, the Netherlands and parts of Germany were predominantly Protestant.

The Catholic Church was not unaware of the different problems that were of major concern to the reformers. In 1545 the Pope called for a general Church council to convene at Trent in northern Italy to deal with the problems that the reformers had raised. The Council of Trent lasted intermittently for eighteen years and dealt with revising the Mass, personal interpretation of Scripture, the role of authority in the Church, the role of faith and good works in man's salvation, and the sacraments. Unfortunately, although Trent was very specific in telling Catholics what to believe, it also seems to have advocated the opposite position from anything the Protestants believed. This diametric opposition to anything Protestant would last for the next four centuries.

In the past three centuries, the Church has been faced with a new series of problems. Religion has largely ceased to hold the important role that it previously had in people's lives. Movements such as humanism, nationalism, and communism have changed the way in which we perceive the world around us. The scientific revolution has totally changed our perception of the universe. No longer do we see ourselves as the pinnacle of creation, but rather as insignificant specks upon a minor planet in an endless universe. Various liberations throughout the world (of women, of races, and of the oppressed) have also affected mankind's relationship to one another and to God. We now live in a world that is constantly changing and moving forward, and this has brought with it a whole different set of issues to which the Church must address itself.

VATICAN II (1962–1965)

Introduction

A general or ecumenical council of the Catholic Church is a gathering of all the bishops in the world who come together to discuss matters of interest to the entire Church. Others may be invited to attend, but it is the bishops who will be the ones to vote on the issues. At the last council the bishops brought along advisors who were able to help update them on theological matters that were being discussed. Representatives from other religions were likewise present as observers. Since the Council of Trent (1545–1563), the Council of Vatican I (1869–1870) had met briefly and defined the controversial question of papal infallibility. Unfortunately its deliberations were cut short by the Franco-Prussian war and its insights into the nature of the Church were aborted. In 1959 Pope John XXIII called for a general council. To many this came as a surprise, but Pope John understood the needs of the times much better than others did.

Background

The Catholic Church was not falling apart in 1959, but the conditions were ripe for a gathering of bishops. A consideration of the following points should show that the needs of the Church in 1959 definitely pointed toward the calling of a council.

Many changes had taken place in the world between 1563 and 1959. People lived a different life-style. The Catholic Church was a worldwide Church and not just a European one. Although the Church was spread all over the world, everyone in a way was so much closer together and conversant with the rest of the world because of the improved communications (travel, radio, TV, etc.). The people in 1959 and today are better educated. There are greater differences between individuals, and their problems are not the same. Pastoral demands as a result are much different.

The knowledge explosion of recent centuries led to new discoveries in all branches of learning. Since all knowledge is related, what happens in one area has its repercussions in other areas. This at times has caused problems, and it certainly has led to a rethinking of one's understanding and expression of knowledge in every area of learning. Some good examples are the impact of science on religion (the God question, the creation of the world, the dignity of man), and of archaeology, history and science upon the proper understanding of the Bible. Truth is one, and all areas must fundamentally be in harmony with each other. Furthermore we have come to realize that truth can be expressed in many ways, each of which has value. Finally, different contexts of living and searching for truth gave rise to different questions and to different answers, even when the questions were quite similar. We ourselves may ask the very same question when we are ten years old, when we are twenty years old, and when we are fifty years old. Each time there is an entirely different situation which throws a new light upon the question and demands a different answer.

Furthermore all kinds of what may be called "ERD" were going on. Throughout the Church lay people, priests and bishops were having new *Experiences* which caused them to *Reflect* upon their Catholic heritage in order to see how the Jesus experience could be best lived and explained today. These experiences and reflections were quite intermingled, each experience affecting other experiences and reflections. In time some *Decisions* on the part of legitimate authority had to be made, but usually these decisions could come about only after long, serious, prayerful reflection. Just a few examples would be these: the liturgy (e.g., celebration of Mass and participation of all), the Bible (and the questions about its proper interpretation raised by the new discoveries in history, archaeology, and science), marriage (birth control, divorce), celibate priesthood, relationships with Protestant churches in ecumenical ventures, philosophical systems (Thomism was not the only one), and the increased attention paid to personalism and its implications for all Christian living.

As a result of these and kindred happenings there was the need for the entire Church to come together (1) to see how to understand God's truth today, (2) to discover how to live together in closer unity and harmony, and (3) to learn how to be of better service to the entire world community.

Stages

A council may be called today, but it does not meet tomorrow. A lot of time is needed to get things ready for a fruitful sharing at a meeting of bishops from all over the world. The following dates summarize this preparatory stage for Vatican II.

Jan. 25, 1959:		Pope John XXIII announced to eighteen cardinals that he was going to call a council and asked them to share their insights with him.
May 17, 1959:		He created a commission or committee to prepare for the council.
June 18, 1959:		Bishops were asked to submit their suggestions as to what topics or issues should be discussed at the council.
July 18, 1959:		Catholic universities were asked to do the same.
June 5, 1960:		Ten commissions or working committees, three secretariats or special offices, and a central commission or committee were established.
Dec. 25, 1961:		The council opening was announced for 1962.
Feb. 2, 1962:		October 11 was set as the opening date.
June 11, 1962:		The central commission in its final meeting retained seventy schemata (or topics) to be discussed. Documents developing them were to be sent to the bishops before the council opened. It is to be noted that not all of these were discussed at the council. Some were dropped; others were combined into one; still others were assigned to different Church offices for consideration and implementation.

| *July 8, 1962:* | All Christian church communities were invited to send observers. |
| *Aug. 6, 1962:* | Operating procedures for the council were set. |

The bishops gathered in Rome and the first session opened on October 11, 1962. The council usually met in general sessions (also called congregations) five days a week. The following was the normal timetable:

9:00–1:00:	Mass followed by the general meeting
1:00–4:00:	Lunch followed by time off for personal business, study, etc.
4:00–7:00:	Meetings of the various commissions or committees which had to work on the various documents. Either during this time or later in the evening there were short-term courses in Scripture, theology, etc., in order to update the bishops on what was going on in the Church's quest for a fuller understanding of revealed truth.

In all, the council met in four sessions, and the accompanying chart gives an overall picture of what took place.

These documents came to see the light of day after a lot of hard work. The fact that so many were approved only in the last session of the council helps to point out that it took time to hammer out a final document.

As was mentioned above, before the council ever opened, suggestions as to what topics or issues should be treated came in from all over the world. These were compiled, combined, accepted, rejected, etc. A preliminary list of "schemata" was drawn up, and copies of documents were made and sent out for reactions. This process of write, circulate, rewrite went on

Session	Dates	General Meetings	Public Sessions	Documents
First	11/11/62–12/8/62	36	1	None
Second	9/29/63–12/4/63	43	2	Liturgy Communications Media
Third	9/14/64–11/21/64	48	2	Church Ecumenism Catholic Churches of Eastern Rites
Fourth	9/14/65–12/8/65	41	5	Revelation Church in Modern World Bishops Religious Life Priests Priestly Formation Laity Missionary Activity Christian Education Religious Freedom Relations with Non- Christian Religions

during the years the council was in existence. At the general meetings of the council the bishops discussed the schemata one by one. Suggestions and strong criticisms were voiced, and then the documents were returned to the commission for revision. This process continued until the assembled bishops were ready for a vote. Three options were available: *yes, yes but* (approving the document with reservations), and *no.*

Changes

The council closed in 1965. Since that time there has been a constant stream of changes that have taken place within the

	BEFORE VATICAN II		AFTER VATICAN II	
	WHYS (INSIGHTS)	**WHATS (PRACTICES)**	**WHYS (INSIGHTS)**	**WHATS (PRACTICES)**
ORGANIZATION	Church is institution monarchy doctrinal system	Monarchial No parish councils Silent laity	Church is mystery community pilgrim people	Priests' senates Due process Consultation of laity
ECUMENISM	Roman Catholic Church is true Church of Jesus Christ Outside the Church no salvation	None No reading of Protestant authors	More than Roman Catholics in body of Christ Freedom of faith Dignity of person	Joint meetings Joint prayer services Seminary consortium Common edition of Bible
LITURGY	Means of salvation Must be performed correctly	Rubrics Uniformity Belonged to priests	Celebration of salvation	Pluralism Vernacular All participate Lay lectors, distributors

Catholic Church. In all truth these changes were not earth-shaking, but to a Church community that had not seen change in four hundred years, every new development did produce upheavals. The results manifested the fact that the Church "teachers" all down the line did not do a very good job of educating their "students" about the changes and why they were made.

For the most part the Church had arrived at deeper insights into the topics or issues discussed (e.g., liturgy, Church, relations with other Christians). These insights then led to changes in Church practice as illustrated in the accompanying chart.

DISCUSSION QUESTIONS

1. Why is it important to have some knowledge of Church history before you understand where the Church is today?

2. Is change necessary? Why didn't the Church remain the same as it was in the first century?

3. What does it mean for Roman Catholics to know their "roots"?

4. Does the Church need a new reformation today? How could such a reformation come about? What direction should it take?

5. If Jesus Christ came on earth today, would he recognize the Church? Why?

6. What changes have taken place in your own parish during your own lifetime?

7. Draw your own personal life-line, indicating the major events, people, etc., that helped to make you what you are today as a Catholic. Indicate the cause-effect relationship that is present.

READINGS

Abbott, Walter, ed. *The Documents of Vatican II.* America, 1966.

Bainton, Roland. *Christendom.* Harper and Row, 1964.

Bausch, William. *Pilgrim Church.* Fides, 1979.

Bokenkotter, Thomas. *A Concise History of the Catholic Church.* Doubleday, 1977.

Day, Edward. *Catholic Church Story.* Liguori, 1975.

McBrien, Richard. *The Remaking of the Church.* Harper and Row, 1973.

O'Connell, Hugh. *Keeping Your Balance in the Modern Church.* Liguori, 1968.

O'Hanlon, David. *What's Happening to the Church?* St. Anthony Messenger, 1974.

2 REVELATION: SCRIPTURE AND TRADITION

Jesus Christ: The Tradition

Catholic faith is based upon the fact of God's revelation. God chose to reveal to us both himself and his plan for our salvation. In doing so he shared with us truths that transcend our human understanding (the Trinity, our call to union with God, the Eucharist, the God-Man, etc.). In the Bible the call of Abraham by God began the whole "story" of man's salvation which culminated in the coming of Jesus Christ. Jesus completed the work of redemption and established the new covenant through which all of us are to be saved.

To assure that his revelation would remain intact with the Christian community down through the ages, God established a teaching office whose task it was to spread the good news to all peoples in all times and places. These first teachers (the apostles) handed on to those who followed them everything necessary for the full living of the Gospel message, but not all was written down in Scripture.

The Catholic community holds that the Holy Spirit, sent by Jesus and the Father, has been present in the Church community down through the ages and is present in the Church today. It is the Spirit who is behind all that is good in this growth and development of the Church, both in its under-standing of the Jesus experience (and this is the basic *tradition* of Christianity), and in the way it expresses this understanding in its moral code, in its creed of beliefs, and in its way of wor-ship centered in the Eucharist. In different times and places these expressions (formulation of beliefs, rituals in worship, customs and practices) or traditions can vary. The lived faith is more important than faith defined or formulated in words.

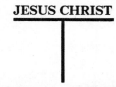

JESUS CHRIST

CHRIST PRESENT IN THE CHURCH NOW

Today the Church community struggles to see how it can best express the Jesus experience as it should be lived today. In seeking greater understanding of the Christ event, the com-munity looks to its past to see how its forebears (the Fathers of the Church, the councils, bishops, etc.) saw Christ and his message. Then it looks to the present to ascertain what insights the bishops, the theologians, and the entire Christian commu-nity today have to offer. The teaching authority of the Church (the magisterium) plays a tempering role and makes certain that all is in line with the "T" in the accompanying chart. Needless to say, there are movements and expressions that may not be the work of the Spirit. It is the role of authority to pass judgment on these new expressions and to see if they do, in truth, manifest the Gospel teaching today.

Thus, in Christianity, Jesus Christ is the central event. Je-sus Christ is the *tradition* that is lived and then passed on by every generation. The first Christians lived with Jesus, prayed with him, listened to him, and marveled at his works. They truly experienced Jesus. Their lives changed as they lived this experience. They were so taken up by it that they had to share it with others—with their families, with their friends, and with the generation to come. The first Christian community gathered together to celebrate these lived memories. This process of living, sharing, and passing on to others their "lived" Jesus experience is what Christianity is all about. The Christian community today should be the living expression of Jesus Christ (with his message), as he (with his message) is experienced and lived today.

Sacred Scripture

The revelation of God is contained partially in Sacred Scripture, written under divine inspiration and teaching what God wants taught. The writers, though, speak in human fashion (literary form, current speech, cultural context, etc.). That is why the Bible is often called the word of God in the words of men. The individuals who wrote the Bible came from a particular time and culture; they thought in that culture's way of thinking and wrote as people of that time might write. We always need to know the total context—historical, cultural, literary—in order to grasp fully the meaning of the texts.

One point to keep in mind, for instance, is literary form— the way of writing or a form of expression that an author chooses for the presentation of his thought. Which one he selects depends upon what he wants to say and why, upon the culture of his times, upon his precise situation in life and history. Just as a newspaper has editorials, cartoons, comics, and news, so an author can select from story, poem, essay, chronicle, history, debate, etc. Christ, for example, used stories or parables to present many of his teachings.

Our understanding of the Bible and biblical texts is so much better and fuller today. Only in the past one hundred and fifty years have cuneiform writings and the hieroglyphics been deciphered so that we could read the literature of the ancient peoples. Further discoveries dealing with their culture and history have been made in the twentieth century (for instance, the Ugarit tablets found in 1930, the Dead Sea Scrolls in 1947, and the Ebla texts in 1974). All of this has thrown a greater light on the Jewish people, their history, their culture, and their writings. Today we know a lot more about the Bible and its peoples than has any previous generation.

In the Old Testament we have the story or account of God's relations with the Jewish people—how he called them out of Egypt and helped them settle in the promised land, how they became a nation and a religious community, and how they gradually grew in their knowledge and worship of the Lord. Step by step we are led up to the coming of Christ.

Catholic editions of the Old Testament divide the forty-five books into twenty-one historical books (Genesis, Exodus, Leviticus, Numbers, Deuteronomy, Joshua, Judges, Ruth, 1 and 2 Samuel, 1 and 2 Kings, 1 and 2 Chronicles or Paralipomenon, Ezra, Nehemiah, Tobit, Judith, Esther, and 1 and 2 Maccabees), seven sapiential or wisdom books (Job, Psalms, Proverbs, Ecclesiastes, Canticle of Canticles, Wisdom, and Sirach or Ecclesiasticus), and seventeen prophetical books (Isaiah, Jeremiah with Lamentations, Baruch, Ezekiel, Daniel and the twelve minor prophets). The Jewish canon, established toward the end of the first century of the Christian era, divides them according to the law, the prophets, and the writings, and does not include Baruch, Sirach, Wisdom, Tobit, Judith, and 1 and 2 Maccabees as well as a few sections of other books. The Protestant editions follow the Hebrew canon but often includes those "omitted" books in an appendix.

The New Testament gives us the life and teachings of Christ and sets forth the fullness of God's plan for man's salvation. It includes the following twenty-seven books: four Gospels (Matthew, Mark, Luke, John), Acts, Apocalypse or

Revelation, and twenty-one epistles (fourteen Pauline, two of Peter, three of John, one of James, and one of Jude).

We should keep in mind that there is a gap between the death of Christ, around 29 A.D., and the writings of the New Testament which we can date roughly from 50 to 100 or even 150 A.D. In a way these writings are the reflected experience of these first Christians. They had seen Christ, heard him, lived with him, and prayed with him. As the years went by they reflected more and more on what all this meant and gradually put it into writing, usually as an answer to a particular question or problem. They are the official testimony and normative expression of this Christ-experience.

Our current knowledge of the New Testament gives us this probable explanation of how a Gospel came to be written. (1) Jesus lived, taught, and performed good works. (2) After Christ's ascension, the early Christian community made daily use of his words and deeds in their liturgies, in their basic preaching of the good news, in their more detailed instructions in the Christian faith, and in deciding many questions on how to live as Christians. (3) As the years went by, the community saw the need to preserve in writing their eye-witness experience of Christ. The evangelists then recorded this tradition, this witness to Christ, and did so in a way suited to the peculiar purpose each one set for himself. Not every Gospel was written for the same kind of community. Thus, we have one Gospel (the life and message of Christ) and many Gospels (accounts of his life according to Matthew, Mark, Luke, and John).

Sacred Scripture is a basic element in living and understanding the full life of the Church. All its teachings, preaching, theology, and prayer life must be nourished by Scripture. Every member of the community should have easy access to the Bible, and all should strive toward a deeper understanding of it. However, not everything that God revealed is contained in the Bible. John himself tells us that there would not be enough books available to contain everything (21:25). The Christian community, guided by the Spirit, passed on from people to people all the basics of Christ's message.

DISCUSSION QUESTIONS

1. When it is said that the Church is a revelation, what do we mean?

2. It is said that in Christianity Jesus Christ is the central event. Do you agree? Why?

3. Should people try to understand the Bible or just live by it? Why?

4. How is the Christian community the living expression of the Gospel of Christ?

5. Could the Church succeed without some form of tradition?

6. Is tradition a beautiful way of expressing continuing faith or a sorry way of clinging to the past?

7. Is the "T" chart a useful symbol for tying together Christ and the Church today?

8. Analyze the daily newspaper and see how it treats the same item in different ways.

READINGS

Congar, Yves. *The Meaning of Tradition.* Hawthorn, 1964.

LaFay, Howard. "Ebla," *National Geographic,* December 1978.

Link, Mark. *Seventh Trumpet.* Argus, 1978.

Link, Mark. *These Stones Shall Shout.* Argus, 1975.

McBrien, Richard. *Who Is a Catholic?* Dimension Books, 1971. Chapter IV.
Moran, Gabriel. *Theology of Revelation.* Herder and Herder, 1966.
O'Collins, Gerald. *Theology and Revelation.* Fides, 1968.
Vatican II. *Constitution on Divine Revelation.*

3 FAITH, THEOLOGY, DOCTRINE

Cardinal Newman once said that if we would define our terms, we would have few arguments. It is very true that in matters of "faith and religion" there have been some violent exchanges because of a lack of understanding of terms and their meaning. The following definitions should help us understand more fully much of what is to come, as well as make us able to handle various writings in the areas of faith, theology, and doctrine.

Faith: Faith is a personal quality that enables us to see reality in a different way, an attitude of a person, a personal attribute that enables us both to *accept* what another says or does (God and his revelation to us) and to *respond* with full commitment of ourselves to this person. This is very much like "love."

Beliefs, Doctrines, Dogma: When faith is looked upon as a creed, as a body of truths, as that which the community believes, we use the term "beliefs." These are called doctrines when they are the officially accepted teachings of a faith community, what is contained in official catechisms. They are called dogmas when they are solemnly defined teachings of a community, such as the dogma of the incarnation, the dogma of the Eucharist, and the dogma of the immaculate conception.

Religion: Religion is an organized religious community with its beliefs, moral code, cult of worship, and organization, such as the Catholic religion.

Theology: Theology has been traditionally defined as "faith seeking understanding." It is the process of reflecting upon my faith experience (both my personal faith and the faith as truths) in order to attain a better understanding of this faith and its beliefs. Note that these beliefs are already the product of a previous act of theology on the part of my predecessors. Every expression of faith (a creed, a council definition, a catechism answer) is a product of theology.

Myth: Myth is an attempt on the part of man to express a truth which the human mind cannot perceive sharply and completely. This may be expressed in a story or in a catechism answer. It is never the final word on the subject. Keep in mind that the formulation of any concept is difficult. We all have trouble saying exactly what we are thinking. When it comes to understanding a mystery (which we really cannot grasp), it is even more difficult to come up with a final formulation in words.

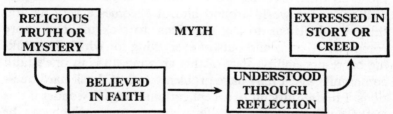

Core-Peripheral: Core truths are basic to the teachings of a faith community and cannot be changed. This does not mean that we cannot arrive at a fuller understanding of this truth, but that the truth itself is an essential part of what makes this community what it is. For example, Jesus is present in the Eucharist. Peripheral truths or facts are items that are are changing and may change tomorrow. These have no great effect on the basic nature of this community—for example, the language in which Mass is celebrated, laws on fast and abstinence, and regulations on intercommunion. In belonging to a community, I cannot deny the core truths, though I may have some questions about them. I can have serious reservations about peripheral items and still remain a faithful member of the community.

CORE/PERIPHERAL

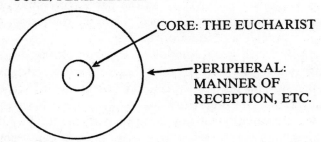

CORE: THE EUCHARIST

PERIPHERAL: MANNER OF RECEPTION, ETC.

Pregnant with Faith: As one grows into adulthood, where the individual becomes responsible for one's total being, as well as for the world around him, it becomes a very natural thing to challenge, to ask questions, to seek to know more completely the ins and outs of everything for which I am taking on responsibility. Part of this growing up is in one's faith community and I may have problems with it. I ask hard questions. I find it difficult to accept certain things. I wonder if this is the community for me. This is a situation which can be termed being "pregnant with an adult faith." There will come the time when the adult faith is born and peace comes. Pregnancy, though, can be troublesome for certain people. At times it helps to have a "spiritual midwife."

Development of Doctrine: The process of growing in one's personal faith and in one's deeper understanding of that faith-experience and the reality it reveals is something that has been going on, likewise, in the faith community which is the Catholic Church. Frequently it is referred to as the development of doctrine. Such development usually involves three elements: experience, reflection, and decision (ERD). Christian people experience problems and challenges in living the Christian life. What does this teaching mean? How do you really live this moral principle today? This leads to reflection on the part of all thinkers in the Church (the Christian people themselves, the professional theologian, the official teacher). Different solutions are offered, comments are made, and insights are given. Since one formulation or decision is not always as good as another, it is the responsibility of authority in the community to sort out these presentations, to evaluate them, and to accept or to reject them as being in conformity or not in conformity with the Christian tradition and the Gospels themselves. It is imperative that such authority be competent. But this interaction of experience, reflection and decision does not usually follow a neat, logical pattern. Even with minimal complications, there is a long time-span between the first experience of the problem and a decision made by authority. Normally, as reflection begins upon one experience, there will be further experiences taking place—some related to this problem, others concerned with a different problem. There will be constant interaction between all the experiences and the reflection. Tentative decisions will be made all along the line. Some solutions will be tossed out immediately as un-Christian. Others may go into the category of "needs another look." Whatever decisions are made will never be the final ones, but just the one for this moment in history. Tomorrow will bring further challenges.

Theology and the Church: As mentioned earlier, *theology* is the process of reflecting upon faith in order to arrive at a fuller understanding of it. In the Church community, the professional theologian is the "R and D" department (research and development). This is where the Church does much of its thinking. Not everyone in the Church has the time and ability to plunge deeply into the study of the problems and questions that develop. It is the professional's task to do this research in a solid, competent manner and then to communicate this to the proper members of the community. At times, the primary thrust of this work is to help explain to the faithful what the Church does teach. On other occasions, it seeks new knowledge so that the Church can teach in a fuller and better way.

Theology and the Individual: All sincere believers must seek a fuller understanding of their faith. All must do some theology. All can profit from a continuing education in their faith—the whole purpose of religious education in grade school, high school, college, and in adult life. There is need for a total parish program in religious education. In this work of continuing education, we need to beware of the "amateur" theologian. Often it is the work of the amateur that has caused trouble in the Church community, as when an amateur presents as solid truth the fruit of his own research. Too often a self-made man can be the product of unskilled labor.

One or many theologies: We are all different, and so are theologians. We look at problems in a slightly different way or come at them from a different vantage point. St. Thomas Aquinas made the intellect and truth his taking-off point. His contemporary, St. Bonaventure, used as his base the will and the good. Their presentations on the Catholic faith did differ, but both presented good insights. To illustrate the differences that may exist between two explanations or approaches to the faith (or theologies) the accompanying settler-pioneer analogy has been used and is quite clear. Each approach is a good one, each says something, but neither tells the whole story. You may have heard the story of an elephant and seven blind men. Each blind man is touching a different part of the elephant (tail, trunk, tusk, leg, etc.) and each is asked to describe what an elephant is. Evidently each tells the truth, but it takes the composite picture of all their stories to come close to the reality. In the same way, different theologies give us different understandings of the faith experience. No one of them is the

	SETTLER	PIONEER
CHURCH	courthouse, town square as a symbol of security, law	covered wagon, always on move, where the action is
GOD	mayor	trail boss, lives and fights with his men
JESUS	sheriff, enforces the rules	scout, finds out the way to go
CHRISTIAN	settler, safety first	pioneer, risk and daring
FAITH	trust in safety of town, obey laws, keep nose clean	spirit of adventure, risk, readiness to move out on trail
SIN	breaking one of town's laws	wanting to turn back

last word on the subject. Theology does not exist without faith, and real faith, seeking to understand itself, cannot exist without theology. Theology, although closely related to faith, is not the faith, nor is it the officially defined teachings of the community. It is the process of understanding the faith and these teachings.

Liberation Theology: Liberation theology comes from Latin America where there are many people who are oppressed and deprived in almost every sense of the word. Deep compassion for them as well as a critical reflection upon their situation in the light of the Gospel of Jesus developed into what is called liberation theology. This is a new approach to theological thinking which clearly points out in a solid manner the need for radical changes in society. It is an attempt to understand the Christian faith which is committed to the liberation of these oppressed peoples. The whole gamut of theological reflection on the basic truths of the Catholic faith is viewed from this point of view of liberation. As a result such basic themes/topics as creation, salvation, sacrament, mission of the Church, etc., take on a new dimension. Because it is linked with the real liberation of an existing oppressed people, it is often looked upon as political and even as having Marxist elements.

DISCUSSION QUESTIONS

1. Are all three parts of the ERD process dependent on each other? Discuss examples which support your answer.
2. Is it possible for theology to exist without faith? Can faith exist without theology?
3. Can a culture exist without myths? Is it always possible to sift the core truth from the myth?
4. Must all sincere believers seek a fuller understanding of their faith?
5. Is there a need for religious education in schools? Should there be any education about religion in the public schools?
6. What is the role of the community in regard to those who are pregnant with faith?
7. When does education in one's faith end?
8. Explain how questioning one's faith may be a sign of a growing faith.

READINGS

Hellwig, Monika. *What Are the Theologians Saying?* Pflaum, 1979. Chapter 1.

McBrien, Richard. "Faith, Theology and Belief," *Commonweal,* November 13, 1974.

McBrien, Richard. *Who Is a Catholic?* Dimension Books, 1971. Chapters II and III.

Weigel, Gustave. *Catholic Theology in Dialogue.* Harper & Row, 1961. Chapter 5.

4 THE NATURE
AND MISSION
OF THE CHURCH

The nature and function of the Church cannot be understood apart from the Christian doctrines of creation and redemption. Just why did God make us? The old catechism answer said: to know him, to love him, to serve him in this life and to be happy with him in the next. Today we might say it in this way: to come to total personal fulfillment by means of all the creatures in this world. We could say that Christ became incarnate in order to save us from our sins, or we might say that it was to show us how to live in this world so as to arrive at total human fulfillment and at a loving friendship with God. Is there a difference in these approaches? Are they mutually exclusive? Can I arrive at total personal fulfillment without knowing, loving and serving God?

Salvation vs. Fulfillment

The Church has no meaning apart from Christ. It is the community he founded, carrying out his mission of building up the kingdom of God and of helping us respond to God's call to enter into a love relationship with him. Is the Church to concentrate upon us as "religious" beings and help us to get to heaven?

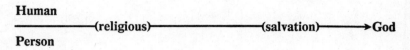

Or is the Church to concentrate upon us as "whole" human beings in the light of our religiosity?

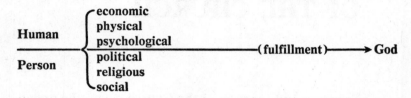

Today more and more emphasis is placed on helping the "whole" person be a true son/daughter of God by living the full human life in this world and helping to establish therein the true kingdom of God. The entire world, not just the people, is God's. The entire creation should give praise and honor to God, but creation can give this only by means of the human race to whom dominion over all the works of creation was entrusted. This explains why the recent Popes and especially Paul VI and John Paul II have so strongly insisted that the Church is on the side of the poor. There is so much more to the work of the Church than Sunday Mass and the sacraments. Even the Mass cannot be understood without reference to the world. The dismissal at the end of Mass sends us out into the world to live what we have celebrated.

Three Views of the Church

As a way of pointing out in graphic detail the differences in the ways one can understand the Church, the following three descriptions may be used. These are just samples and are not meant to be the only ones.

GHETTO CHURCH

The "Ghetto Church" is a closed community within which its members live and act. The main job of the Church is to make its members *holy.* It is to teach them what Christ taught, to rule them according to his laws, to sanctify them through his sacraments. It is to concentrate on its own members and on converts who come into its community. It is not concerned about the world outside.

"R AND R" CHURCH

The "R & R" (Rest and Recreation) Church recognizes that there is that separate, un-Christian world into which its members go to work and to play, but they have to return to the Church in order to be re-created as Christians. The Church fulfills the function of making holy as above, but it also has to *teach* its members so that they can help Christianize that outside world. In this way the world will contaminate them less and less. Note that the members do the Christianizing; the Church itself is not directly involved.

LEAVEN CHURCH

The "Leaven Church" considers the Church as a part of the entire world that is to be made into the kingdom of God. The Church is in the world, and all members of the Church work as a leaven within the world. All peoples are part of the mission of the Church; all facets of human living are included. The Church is intimately related to everything. Thus, in addition to the above functions of making holy and teaching, the Church is to *serve* the entire world. It is involved in the whole world—in economics, in politics, and in other spheres. It speaks out (both priests and lay members);

it acts (marches on picket lines, runs for political office, publishes newspapers). It does not just stay in the church and in the church schools. It is not afraid to champion the cause of the poor and the disadvantaged. It works to bring about a change in society so that the rights of all peoples are respected.

It is the Church under this third description that is coming to the fore today. All Church documents, from Vatican II's *Constitution on the Church in the Modern World* to the declarations of the Latin American Bishops at Puebla in 1979, emphasize the commitment of the Church to the poor and to working toward the eradication of those conditions which cause such poverty. There is naturally a difference of opinion as to how this should be done and as to the correct role of the clergy. Statements by Pope John Paul II make it clear that politics is not the domain of the clergy or religious.

Models of the Church

In searching out a deeper understanding of the Church today, Avery Dulles came up with a number of different ways of looking at the Church, each of which has its own contribution to make. Among other models, the Church may be viewed as:

- Institution: We are an organized community with structures, e.g., hierarchy, sacraments, Mass, laws.
- Communion: We are the people of God called together to share in his gifts coming to us from the Spirit.
- Sacrament: We are a visible manifestation of the redeeming grace of Christ that is given to all people.
- Herald: We proclaim the Gospel message to the entire world.
- Servant: We are for all others. We are to serve the individual and social needs of all peoples.

Church as Community

One of the models which has received a great amount of attention today is looking upon the Church as a community. A community may be defined as a fellowship of individuals, bonded together in the Spirit, with common ideals and goals, sharing all they have and being responsible for each and for all. A fellowship is something stable, larger than any individual; it has its own history and tradition. Bonded together in the Spirit shows that it is a close-knit group of believers in God who are committed to his kingdom which is to be established. They share in everything they possess, in everything they have to do—all in proportion to their personal talents. Each is responsible for self, for each other, for the total community, and for the realization of the community's goals and purposes. Such a view of the Church helps us to understand in a fuller manner such things as the following, and many others as well.

- Jesus Christ is the basic experience of this community.
- The Christian tradition is the living of the Jesus experience today.
- We have a basic creed of beliefs about God, man, and the world.
- Baptism is the initiation rite into the community.
- The Mass is the community gathered together to worship the Lord in a fitting manner.
- Our moral code is a close following of Christ who invites us to a full life of love.
- There is an organization which enables us to use all we have and all we can do for the good of all the peoples of the earth.
- In order to share what our community is all about, we have a solid program of religious education for every member of the community.

Every aspect of the Church is seen in a different light, and the end result is a fuller grasp of what it means to be a Christian in this faith community.

The question of why an organized community comes up again and again. In answer to this, Robert McAfee Brown shares some excellent insights with us. In the first place, it enables both the faith of the community and the faith of the individual to be tested. The community with its longer history and memory tests the faith of the individual; the latter, with the leaven of new ideas, tests the faith of the group. Next, since faith does involve risk, the community supports and strengthens individuals who are "pregnant with faith." Further, the liturgy, which takes place only in community, enables us to celebrate and to embody our vision of faith as something that exists now and not just as a future hope. More will be said on this when we discuss the Eucharist. Finally, all good things are fruitful; any real community is missionary. We spread the good word, not as a solo venture, but together, whether this be as a duet, a trio, or an entire chorus.

DISCUSSION QUESTIONS

1. Do you see any problems arising in an open Church which is open to all peoples, all truths, and all approaches to truth?

2. What is your definition of "Church"? How does this definition compare with your definition of community?

3. Why is it important that the Church be an organized community rather than an individual experience?

4. Is the Church primarily to make man "holy" or to make him "whole"?

5. Should the Church send missionaries to convert other cultures or should the "leaven" in our community be allowed to spread naturally throughout the world?

6. Every community has institutions, but not every institution is a community.

7. Does the Church have a place in politics?

READINGS

Buhlmann, Walter. *The Coming of the Third Church.* Orbis, 1977.

Clark, Stephen. *Building Christian Communities.* Ave Maria, 1972.

Delespesse, Max. *The Church Community: Leaven and Life Style.* Ave Maria, 1968.

Dulles, Avery. *Models of the Church.* Doubleday, 1974.

Dulles, Avery. *The Resilient Church.* Doubleday, 1977.

John Paul II. *Redeemer of Man.* March 4, 1979.

Pfeifer, Carl. *Teaching the Church Today.* Twenty-Third Publications, 1978.

Rahner, Karl. *The Shape of the Church to Come.* Seabury, 1972.

Rahner, Karl. *Christian at the Crossroads.* Seabury, 1975.

Vatican II. *Constitution on the Church.*

Vatican II. *Constitution on the Church in the Modern World.*

5 THE ORGANIZATION OF THE CHURCH

At the very beginning the Catholic Church was an informal and loosely organized religious community. As the Church spread throughout the Mediterranean world and as it took upon itself various tasks and services, the organization became more set and more complex. The centuries have added to this so that today, both in Rome (the central government of the Church) and in the individual diocese, the organization of the Church resembles that of most bureaucracies.

To discuss the organizational structure of the entire Church would demand a book all by itself. All we want to do here is to give a very general overall view with some specific illustrations (Chart I on the next page).

The Pope is the head of all. The bishops of the various countries band together as the group that sets policies, etc., for the Church in that country. Here in the United States the Church is divided into various provinces, composed of the dioceses of one or more states. Each diocese is broken down into deaneries, and these in turn are divided into various parishes.

The papal curia which assists the pope is a large, complex structure, including various Congregations (e.g., for Catholic Education, for Divine Worship), Secretariats (e.g., for Christian Unity, for Non-Believers), Tribunals (e.g., Sacred

CHART I

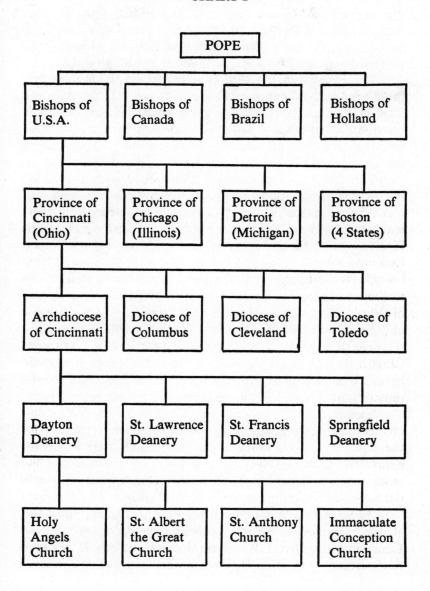

Roman Rota), Offices (e.g. General Statistics Office, Prefecture of the Papal Household), and Commissions (e.g., for Biblical Studies, for Revision of Canon Law, for Latin America). Just reading the list of these various offices and what they do is mind-boggling. It makes one think of Washington, D.C.

The bishops of the U.S. have organized themselves into the National Conference of Catholic Bishops. It provides the bishops with an opportunity to get together on a regular basis in order to share their insights and experiences. Through their meetings and through the various committees the NCCB is able as a group to exercise the pastoral office of the bishop.

The United States Catholic Conference is sponsored by the NCCB. It was founded to assist the bishops in their work, and it provides the necessary organizational structure for the operations of the Church on a national or interdiocesan level. A listing of all these structures can be found in *The Catholic Directory*.

On the diocesan level the story is similar to that of the Roman curia but on a milder scale. Each bishop has various officials to help in the general overall "running" of the diocese, and much of the work is assigned to various Offices and Commissions (e.g., Education, Hospitals, Charities, Priests' Personnel Board). The larger the diocese, the more complex becomes the administrative structure. Many dioceses now have priests' senates functioning; their main purpose is to help set policy for the diocese.

On the parish level today more and more people are involved in the overall work of the parish and share in the responsibilities. These include not only the pastor and his assistants, but also such people as the school principal, youth minister, and the religious education director.

Although the basic structures exist in theory, not every parish has a well-functioning council, nor does every diocese have a viable senate. The structures are there both to take care of the needs of this body (parish, diocese, etc.) and also to al-

CHART II

	Pope	Cardinal	Bishop	Pastor
How Chosen	Elected by cardinals in closed session	Appointed by Pope	Appointed by Pope, usually with consultation	Appointed by bishop aided by personnel board
Qualifications	Any male Catholic, usually a cardinal	Bishop or priest; last layman in 1876	Thirty years old; five years a priest; usually theologian or canonist	Priest with leadership, moral character, administrative talents
Powers	Supreme teacher, lawgiver, pastor; makes all appointments	Elect Pope	Teacher and lawgiver in diocese	Limited jurisdictional power; usual power of any priest
Duties	Oversees work of curia and bishops; pastor of whole Church	Bishops of dioceses, heads of curial offices	Guide and administrator for diocese; confirms; ordains priests	Administers sacraments, preaches, teaches, promotes good works, leads community
Aided By	Cardinals, curia, synods of bishops, general council		Senate of priests, diocesan synods, chancery officials	Priests, parish council, lay ministers, parishioners

low for "all" members to take part in the overall responsibilities by making decisions and carrying them out. How this
functions in real life depends upon local circumstances.

Very often questions are asked about the offices of Pope,
cardinal, bishop, and pastor. Chart II endeavors to answer
some of these basic questions. For more information about
specific items, other sources (e.g., *New Catholic Encyclopedia*)
should be consulted.

6 AUTHORITY

In seeking to understand the complete meaning and responsibility of authority, theologians ask this question: Does authority reside only in the Popes and bishops, or in the entire community? The thrust of Vatican II (and of much of the long tradition in the Church) was that it resided in the entire community. The problem usually revolves around how the members of the community exercise their authority. The structures of both parish and diocesan councils help. The opportunity for dialogue and consultation enables people to have their say. However, it is never going to be a question of putting things to a vote.

As Christ incarnate today, the Christian community has one basic mission: to serve the world after the example of Christ and in doing so to witness to the *truth* of Jesus Christ in its creeds, in its moral code, in its cult of worship, in its services, in its teaching, in its acting, in what it *is* and in what it *does.*

Authority helps the Church to be faithful to this mission and should be viewed as a function, as a responsibility, not as an office or position of honor. Authority denotes leadership, helping the community to realize its mission to truth and to service. The ones in authority must be leaders and not policemen who function to correct those who make mistakes. Authority must be apostolic—faithful to the witness of the apostles in their exercise of authority.

Whenever you have a community you have someone in charge. Peter exercised leadership among the apostles. The Pope did likewise in the Christian community of the early centuries. The same is true today. If we keep in mind our own experiences of holding office in various organizations, we see right away the function of authority—to lead, and to do the work. That is why a title given to the Pope truly describes his function: Servant of the Servants of God.

The Christian community, which has this function of bearing witness to the truth of Jesus Christ, is aptly described as a pilgrim Church, "semper reformanda." The truth resides in a community that is growing, developing, evolving. The truth possessed is not yet the fullness of truth, but "on the way." There is the absence of some truth, or certainly the absence of the full understanding of truth, and perhaps, at times, the presence of some error.

The community bears witness to truth, having been charged with the mission of preaching the Gospel of Jesus Christ to all peoples and teaching them all that he has taught the community. This is no easy task. Refer back to the development of the Church's understanding of itself and of the teachings that have been given to it, and you will recall that it is an on-going as well as difficult process. Each age brings with it its own problems and challenges. Just what is the Christian voice to say today, and who is to be the speaker?

There is a difference in speakers. Consider the following cases: the Pope addressing the entire Church in an encyclical letter, a bishop sending a pastoral letter to be read in all churches in his diocese, a local pastor preaching the Gospel on a Sunday morning, a mother talking to her children, and a third-grader telling his kid brother what he learned in religion class. As you go up the ladder, the speaker carries more weight.

The Magisterium

It is true that the entire community does participate in the teaching function of the Church. We are all teachers and we are all learners. We have to know before we can teach. But someone in the community has to be the official spokesman. "Magisterium," the term used to identify this teaching office of the Church, has traditionally meant the Pope and the bishops as the official teachers of the Church. The magisterium plays its own unique role in proclaiming the Gospel; no other member or members of the Church community can do what these official teachers do. Although at times the magisterium does have to step in to settle disputes or to point out that someone is expressing views that are not in harmony with this community's tradition, its role is much broader than this. Its on-going task is always to seek out and to make known what the *tradition* (the Jesus experience) is today—to make Christ alive and present in this community's teaching and living today. It is both a learning magisterium (that studies, dialogues, listens, and shares) and a teaching magisterium (that takes the time and effort to become a good teacher).

The magisterium, as a good teacher, must know the material and still continue to learn. A good teacher is aware of the needs of the students and usually seeks to enlighten them rather than to prove personal superiority and make demands upon them. There is a big difference in the demands made by good *teaching* and the demands made by a *teacher*. A good teacher does not overteach. No matter how competent the teacher, though, there will always be problems and challenges both because of the subject matter taught and because of the nature of the students themselves.

Problems can be very complex with no easy or set answer. Many issues in the Church today show this—for example, divorce and remarriage, celibate clergy, women priests, homosexual behavior, celebration of the Mass and sacraments,

Catholic education, the relation between bishops and universities, and liberation of the poor. And then students are always students. There is a big difference in teaching a class of fifteen homogeneous students vitally interested in the topic at hand and a mixed class of forty students. These latter will differ in their personal background and preparation for the class, in their interest in the material, in their attentiveness, and in their being prepared for this class session. Being the teacher of a worldwide community such as the Catholic Church is not an easy task.

Every good teacher likewise knows the benefits that come from challenging students. They keep the teacher alert; they lead all to greater heights of understanding of the material, and to greater preparedness for the class meeting. All good students must be willing and able to ask questions, and to challenge the teacher when the material is not understood or perhaps not presented clearly. This is the mark of a good learning situation and all good teachers relish it. Students in the Church community should act in the same way, challenging and questioning, but always in a respectful manner, befitting one who is seeking the truth and not the personal limelight.

DISCUSSION QUESTIONS

1. Must we have authority to survive?
2. How can we equip ourselves for our role as teachers? What are our responsibilities as teachers in this faith community?
3. Should authority be given only to those in the priesthood?
4. Discuss how authority is distributed in your parish (i.e., among priests, principal, parish council) and compare it with other parishes.
5. Is there sufficient authority at the parish level to en-

able the Church to respond adequately to local issues? Should the Catholic Church be a democracy?

6. How do we lay people exercise our authority in the faith community?

READINGS

Baum, Gregory. "Magisterium in a Changing Church," *Concilium,* Volume 21, Paulist, 1967.

Daniélou, Jean. *Why the Church?* Franciscan Herald, 1974.

Dulles, Avery. *The Survival of Dogma.* Doubleday, 1974.

McBrien, Richard. *Who Is a Catholic?* Dimension Books, 1971. Chapter V.

McCord, Peter. *A Pope for All Christians?* Paulist, 1976.

McKenzie, John. *Authority in the Church.* Sheed and Ward, 1966.

Rahner, Karl. "Theology and the Magisterium After the Council," *Theology Digest,* Sesquicentennial Issue, 1968.

7   INFALLIBILITY

Vatican Council I (1869–1870) was called during a time of trial and tribulation. Italy was unified and the papal states were lost. Liberalism and Marxism were gaining steam. The Church and the papacy were not at the height of their power and prestige. The Council's deliberations were cut short by the Franco-Prussian War, and the full examination of the Church and its authority was not completed. The Council was able to discuss the teaching authority of the Pope and came up with the following definition of infallibility:

> The Roman Pontiff, when he speaks *ex cathedra,* that is, when, in the discharge of the office of pastor and doctor of all Christians, by virtue of his supreme apostolic authority he defines a doctrine regarding faith or morals to be held by the universal Church, by the divine assistance promised to him in blessed Peter, is possessed of that infallibility with which the divine Redeemer willed that his Church should be endowed for defining doctrine regarding faith and morals: and therefore such definitions are irreformable of themselves and not from the consent of the Church.

Over the years this definition was not always correctly understood and the authority of the Pope was often exaggerated. In recent decades it had almost come to the point that anything the Pope said was infallible and had to be accepted as such. One modern theologian, Yves Congar, has referred to this tendency toward maximalization as "creeping infallibility." It is true that the Pope as official teacher of the entire Church must be listened to with respect and obedience. What he says should be accepted, but always with an inquiring mind.

Christ promised to confirm his community (the Church) in truth and said that he would send his Spirit to see that this was done. This confirmation in truth refers to the entire community, but the magisterium, as an official teacher, occupies a special place and function. (See Mt 16:18; 18:18; Lk 22:32.) Though the whole community may hold or even teach an infallible truth, they are not empowered juridically to do so infallibly. Strictly speaking, since 1870 only the Pope formally does this. It is true that when the bishops throughout the world agree on a matter of faith (or morals, in rare special cases) they are thought to do so infallibly, but this is, of course, a bit more "diffused" than a papal statement. Whenever the Pope proclaims something infallibly, he is actually proclaiming what the people of God already believe; he does not dig up something new. It must already be a part in some way of that basic "tradition" of the Church community. (See Chapter 2.) This infallibility of the papal magisterium is the same as the infallibility Christ wished his Church to have.

The Pope is infallible only under certain conditions:

- His teaching must concern the teachings of the Gospels (necessary for salvation); it must be a question of faith or morals. Vatican I debated extensively the meaning of "morals" and what was included. The council fathers agreed that it included whatever is needed to protect revelation, but they did not agree on specifics. Questions like inflation, nuclear disarmament, and nuclear power plants, though of great importance, would not be included.

- He must address the entire Church community and not just a part of it.
- He must explicitly state that what he is saying is binding, to be believed by all.
- He must speak *ex cathedra*, i.e., as official teacher of the entire Church.

Infallibility is not an absolute power belonging to the Pope as a person, though at the moment of definition he personally exercises it. It belongs to the office and not to the person. It is never absolute. The Pope, just as the entire Church, is always subject to Scripture, to the word of God. He must consult the faith of the entire Church whenever he wishes to teach authoritatively. He teaches what is already a part of that on-going tradition in the Church. He can teach infallibly only those truths that are necessary for salvation—the basics of the Gospel message.

Infallible statements do not depend upon numerical acceptance in order for them to be infallible. The majority does not rule; truth does. In proclaiming a truth—for instance, that Jesus is truly God and truly man—the Church states what is. There was a time in the early Church when Arianism (which held that Jesus was less than the Father) may have had more adherents than did the Catholic Church which hammered out and then held on to the definitions of Nicaea and other early councils. But the councils were correct, and truth did win out in the end. The council fathers at Nicaea based their definition of the divinity of Christ (he was one in being with the Father) on the Scriptures. If even a majority were to go against the evident sense of Scripture, they would not be right. Jesus promised his followers the Holy Spirit, the Spirit of truth, who would make clear what he had taught. Infallible statements represent the truth of revelation; they are based on Scripture and affirmed by the whole Church under the guidance of the Holy Spirit.

Infallible pronouncements are rare and come for a reason—to answer a serious question/problem/heresy, or to give guiding insights to Christian living. In addition to the definition of infallibility at Vatican I, there have been only two other infallible declarations in the past two centuries: that of the immaculate conception in 1854, and that of the assumption of Mary in 1950.

DISCUSSION QUESTIONS

1. Would the Church or the papacy be anything less if the Pope were not infallible?
2. Must the "Church" be infallible?
3. Explain how, even without infallibility, the Catholic Church would always have a teaching authority with the Pope as its head.
4. Will there be future infallible statements?
5. Every religious community has some statements/presuppositions which it considers infallible.

READINGS

Heft, James, "Papal Infallibility and the Union of Christians," *Catholic Mind,* October 1979.

Hellwig, Monika. *What Are the Theologians Saying?* Pflaum, 1970. Chapter 3.

Kirvan, John, ed. *The Infallibility Debate.* Paulist, 1971.

McBrien, Richard. *Who Is a Catholic?* Dimension Books, 1971. Chapter VI.

8 RESPONSIBLE DISSENT

Within the Church community dissent is always possible and perhaps, at times, necessary. We are all the Church and we all have our roles to play. We need to be responsible and to respect one another as well as help one another fulfill our respective roles in the community. (Cf. ERD in Chapter 3.) Each can be right and each can be wrong; each has something to contribute. Dialogue is important.

After the appearance of the so-called "birth control" encyclical, *Humanae Vitae,* in July 1968, there was a loud roar of dissent throughout the Catholic community. Not all of it was responsible. In each country the bishops got together and issued pastoral letters to their people, endeavoring to help them both understand the encyclical and respond to it in a proper way. The Belgian bishops had this to say about a proper response to the teaching authority of the Church:

- Every doctrinal declaration of the Church should be received with respect and docility.
- Infallible pronouncements must be adhered to with obedience of faith.
- Non-infallible teachings demand, in principle, a religious submission of will and mind, which is based on authority, not on the arguments used.
- Competent individuals may, after serious examination

before God, come to other conclusions but must be sincerely disposed to continue their inquiry, adhere to Christ and the Church, respect the teaching authority of the Pope, and beware of compromising the common good.

- Some of the faithful may not see how they can conform. They must loyally seek the best Christian way of acting and constantly remain open to a better response.

Thus we may conclude that no sincere Roman Catholic may disregard the magisterium. Dissent is possible, but it must be responsible. Answers to the basic questions of who, what, when, where, by what means, why and how should give us a good picture of what this means.

- Who may dissent? Is dissent limited to professionals only? The answer is "no." Every member, insofar as he or she is competent, may dissent. We need to be careful. Many of us have a tendency to exaggerate our own capabilities, especially when the problems concern us.
- About what can I dissent? Are there limitations to the areas about which I may dissent? Again, the answer will depend upon personal competence. Am I truly competent in this particular matter, or is it that I just don't want to measure up to a challenge?
- When, where, and by what means can I dissent? This is hard to pinpoint, but what I do should be appropriate. I don't necessarily dissent with the preacher in the pulpit during the service. I do not necessarily call a press conference. If I am acting responsibly, I shall have respect for all concerned and act accordingly.
- Why am I dissenting? Is it for the true growth of myself and of the community, or is it a personal vendetta, a prideful self-seeking or a refusal to measure up?
- How do I dissent? The answer is simple—responsibly.

This involves, first of all, respect for authority. I must presume that authority used all apt means and had good reasons for the decisions made. I must present their case fairly and adequately. Too often we fail to do this. On the other hand, I have to have care for the less competent. I can cause harm to some people who are not as qualified as I am. Furthermore, I need to have due regard for the gravity of the matter. I need serious and well-founded reasons for my dissent, and since I am dealing with a faith community, I should not dissent before I have spent sufficient time in prayerful reflection. Lastly, I should be motivated by a search for the fullness of the truth and should not be on some kind of ego trip.

At this point, it should be easy to see why education in one's faith is important, why one must continue to study one's religion, why there must be good adult religious education programs, and why we should make ourselves acquainted with all the teachings of a Church community and not neglect certain ones (especially the social teachings on peace and justice for all people).

Stages of Relating

Combining the two concepts of "pilgrim" and "pregnant with faith" we come to see that as individuals in a faith community, we can be pregnant with faith more than once as we grow from childhood into the full maturity of old age. Further, at any one time we are not at the same stage on every point of belief and practice of the community. Keeping these thoughts in mind, the accompanying chart should throw some light on the situation of questioning, challenging, and dissenting.

1	2	3	4	5	6	7
accept	fidget	clarify	question	challenge	dissent	leave

When they are young and growing up, most community members totally accept the community, its teachings, and its standards, and they are very comfortable in such a position. In the second stage we feel uneasiness about some things but are not able to pinpoint them sufficiently well so that we can ask questions. In the third stage we do ask questions but mainly for clarification purposes. We accept the answers quite readily. In our fourth stage we ask more serious questions. We even question the answers given to us as we enter into dialogue and disagreement. In the fifth stage we seriously challenge the Church's position. We find it very difficult to accept its teachings on a certain point. In our dialogue with the community we disagree strongly, but we still remain a member. In the sixth stage we come to dissent. After serious, prayerful reflection, and dialogue with competent people, we are convinced that we are right and we dissent. We may choose to keep our dissent quiet or we may make it known. In either case we may still decide that even though we are right, we shall remain in the community while we work toward the growth of the Church community to a fuller understanding of the issue at hand. The Church is *semper reformanda* (always in need of reform). Finally we come to stage seven where we so strongly disagree with the community and that for which it stands that we have to leave. This last stage is not reached by too many.

There are various areas that illustrate the above stages. In the area of morality there are the questions of premarital sex, abortion, birth control, remarriage after divorce, and the social teachings of the Church. In the area of Church discipline you have the eucharistic fast, Sunday Mass, and celibacy. We would not want to say, though, that every dissenter is right.

In these cases there is an established Church teaching or practice. The ERD process is challenging this, and a certain amount of serious dialogue is taking place. When there are new areas to explore, someone has to do the pioneering and be at the cutting edge of experience which may or may not be in accord with the established teaching or practice. A general rule to follow could be to abide by community rule until a change is made, unless one has very solid reasons for going ahead. These should be in proportion to the point at hand. The important questions to ask are: Am I willing to change if I am proven wrong? Am I truly pioneering or just self-seeking?

Who is right and who is wrong? Normally, abiding by the community practice is best and is correct, but it is difficult to say that each one who disagrees and has experiences on the cutting edge of the things is wrong. These very experiences lead to the challenges and possibly to growth. However, there is need to be very responsible here. We need great competence, and we must be seeking the good of the community and not our own selfish good. No matter which decision is made, most probably some mistakes are going to occur, but if we all are truly seeking the good of the community, truth will win out in the end.

DISCUSSION QUESTIONS

1. When dissenting, what are some of the considerations about ourselves that we must take into account? Discuss how we could rate our competence.

2. How can we tell responsible dissent from irresponsible dissent?

3. Does the Church requirement that a dissenter be "competent" mean that Church officials can ignore opposing views within the Church?

4. If the Church is teaching and preaching the truth, why should anyone wish to dissent?

5. Although dissenting during a Sunday service would probably not be called responsible, it would call the community's attention to the problem. Would the end outweigh the means and bring about a better understanding?

6. Does continuing one's religious education increase the chance of responsible dissent?

7. How can dissent aid in the development of the Church?

8. Does responsible dissent look for a reaction or for a solution?

READINGS

Arzube, Juan. "Criteria for Dissent in the Church," *Origins,* May 11, 1978.

Congar, Yves. *Challenge to the Church: The Case of Archbishop Lefebvre.* Our Sunday Visitor, Inc., 1976.

McBrien, Richard. *Who Is a Catholic?* Dimension Books, 1971. Chapter V.

9 THE CHURCH: A WORSHIPING COMMUNITY

The worship life of the Church community is usually that part of the Church's life that is most visible to many people. It is an area which reflects in its own changes the newer insights into faith and salvation gained by a community. Those pregnant with faith often have problems with the worship life of the community (Mass, confession, etc.).

Worship occurs in a community that believes in God, that searches to relate to God, that responds to the felt presence of God in this community. Recognizing our God for what he truly is, we desire to offer him the very best that we have. Only the very best will satisfy our need to respond to God who has allowed himself to be experienced by us.

Religion should never remain merely a private affair. True religion forms fellowship, community, and togetherness. Where religion is alive, people seek to share this aspect of their lives. I can always pray privately. As a member of the social group, I also want to worship God with this community of believers. We all believe in God. We want to come together to share this belief, to share our love, to acknowledge our relationship, and to manifest our gratitude and our deep commitment to him. In group worship there is always something present (this social element) that is not there in private prayer. Seeing a movie with a really close friend is not the same as seeing it by myself. There is a sharing of two people that is more than just the sum total of the two individuals; the togetherness and response it evokes from each adds something. Since worship is giving the best I have, I want to give this something extra as well as all the private praying that I might want to do.

A particular Church community will regulate its worship in some way. It will determine *the* way *this* community will *officially* worship. It can require attendance at certain worship events as a manifestation of one's real understanding of this community and of one's personal commitment to it. In the Catholic Church there is the official worshiping of the Lord that takes place in the Sunday celebration of the Eucharist.

All too often our history tells us that the Church community failed to instruct its members properly as to the whys and wherefores of what is done in worship. When we gather to celebrate but do not know why we are there or why we are doing what we are doing, the celebration ceases to be a celebration and becomes some mechanical operation, and we may soon become disenchanted. Changes in the structures of the celebration bring no lasting improvement. Those present need to know why they are there and what they are doing. The same is true when there is a question of people who became very attached to the ways things were done and hate to give them up—for instance, Latin in the liturgy, the quiet Mass, etc. These people too need to be educated in the meaning of the new ways and the new expressions of the age-old tradition.

Liturgy

Liturgy is the "celebration of presence." It is the creative use of words and actions, and especially of symbol, to tell the story of who and what we are and thus make Christ present in our midst. We then celebrate.

All important celebrations are organized. Ritual is the organizing of words, actions, and things in order to celebrate something meaningful to the community—July 4, Thanksgiving, New Year's Eve, Mass. We use the basics through which man communicates with his fellow man: words, acts (handshake, embrace, wave of the hand), and symbols (flag, ring, water, food and drink). In liturgy we make ample and creative use of signs, and especially of symbols. Traffic lights and road signs are just that—signs. They convey information (stop, one way, sharp curve) and end there. Symbols such as a flag, a cross, an embrace, or a "meal" convey a meaning which is very deep; they get at the mystery involved; they evoke a response from us.

A flag makes me think of my country. I think of the U.S.A. and its ideals, what it stands for: freedom, opportunity, rights of every person, no privileged class. I recall my relationship to this country, and feelings of patriotism come forth— I'm proud to be a part of it, I salute it, I pledge allegiance. I give of myself to this country and to this community. The cross makes me think about Jesus Christ dying for all of us because he loved me. It makes me think about my own dignity. There is a God who created me, who loved me, who died for me, who makes demands of me, who does not throw me away when I make a mistake, who wants to help me grow as a real "lover," who wants me to repent, to be converted and to love all the more. An embrace is not just a physical contact. It is many things. It says I love you, I care for you, I'm glad you are here; you make me want to do better; you comfort me, you strengthen me, you challenge me. A family meal is so much more than a cafeteria. It is a gathering of loved ones, involving closeness, togetherness, bonds of love and friendship. It is a sharing of time, of conversation, of selves over a meal. Ordinarily not the menu but being there and sharing is the most important thing. (In the Eucharist the "menu" is very important, but it, too, must be seen in light of the community.)

Good liturgy revolves around the creative use of all these human instruments—of silence (so that we can reflect on what has been said or done), of words (especially the words of the One whose presence we are celebrating), of music (which can express the fullness of our being and emotions so much better than the word all by itself), of gestures (which, like pictures, are worth a thousand words), and of symbols (the togetherness and union expressed in a family meal).

What the liturgy is doing through these organized rituals is to tell a story—in reality *the* story of who we are as children of God redeemed by God's Son. In brief, it is the story of the "Christ event." This is done in the celebration of all the sacraments, but especially in the Mass or Eucharist where the full story of what Christianity is all about (the Christ event) is told and celebrated liturgically.

Liturgy thus makes present, here in our midst, Jesus himself. A person can be physically present in his flesh and blood, and also be symbolically present. We make loved ones present by a picture on our desk, or by carrying a memento around. Liturgically by telling "the story" of Christianity we make present, right here and now, the very events that form the story. With Jesus present here in our midst we who believe in him can do nothing else but celebrate. Our Lord is alive and here with us. That is why we call liturgy the celebration of presence. It is an honor to be there.

Sacraments

In our lives as Christians this celebration of Christ's presence will be there all through our existence. By means of the sacraments the Church community celebrates the presence of Christ as we are brought into the community (baptism and confirmation). We grow in the life of grace by eating and drinking (the Eucharist). We are healed and reconciled when we fail to measure up to the community's standards (confession or reconciliation). We enter into specific states of life as a priest or as a married person (holy orders, matrimony). In time of sickness and death we have the healing consolation of the Lord (anointing of the sick).

These sacraments are special but very real ways in which Christ is truly present and through which the faithful believer has real, though sacramental, contact with Christ. Something deeply spiritual does happen, and the sacrament both causes it and expresses it. The sacraments focus God's grace on special moments of our lives. In subsequent sections most of them will be treated in detail.

The Liturgical Year

The Church is a teacher as well as a celebrator. In its liturgical celebrations throughout the year it lives the entire life of Christ so as each year to call to our attention what Christianity is all about. During the four weeks of Advent the Church relives the entire Old Testament time of waiting and preparing for the coming of the Messiah. At Christmas it celebrates the birth of the Savior and the various events that took place then. During Lent it relives the years of public ministry of the Lord and helps the Christian both to realize and to measure up to the challenge of following Christ. The dramatic events of the week, beginning with Passion Sunday (formerly called Palm Sunday) and ending with Easter, the feast of the resurrection, bring out the death-life theme in the life of every Christian. In the Sundays of the ordinary year between Christmas and Lent it reminds us of our baptismal commitment as it celebrates the baptism of Christ and the beginning of his ministry. After the season of Easter culminating in the ascension and Pentecost (the descent of the Holy Spirit), the Church celebrates the risen life of Christ in heaven and on earth present in us, the Christian community, who are living the Christ event today. This reliving of the life of Christ throughout the year is called the liturgical year.

DISCUSSION QUESTIONS

1. Discuss why believing members of a faith community include both social and private prayer in their worship life.

2. Why do we need to encounter (meet) Christ before we can become interested in celebrating his presence?

3. Analyze a non-liturgical celebration (birthday, graduation, July 4, etc.) and show how it has been organized to celebrate something meaningful.

4. Is it true that in worship life, just as in everyday life, those who love celebrate best? Why?

5. Why must every faith community have some kind of community worship?

6. Discuss how the way in which a community worships together says a lot about the state of prayer in the lives of the individual members of the community.

7. Discuss in detail the differences between sign and symbol. Give examples.

READINGS

Champlin, Joseph. *The Sacraments in a World of Change.* Ave Maria, 1973.

Davis, Charles. *Liturgy and Doctrine.* Sheed and Ward, 1961.

Gelineau, Joseph. *The Liturgy Today and Tomorrow.* Paulist, 1978.

Hellwig, Monika. *The Meaning of the Sacraments.* Pflaum, 1972.

Padavano, Anthony. *Presence and Structure.* Paulist, 1976.

Vatican II, *Constitution on the Sacred Liturgy.*

10 INITIATION INTO THE COMMUNITY: BAPTISM AND CONFIRMATION

History of Baptism

Matthew (28:19) and Mark (16:15) tell us that Christ's final parting word to his apostles instructed them to go out and baptize all peoples, teaching them all that he had taught them. Down through the ages Christian churches have been carrying out this command.

From the very first centuries both baptism of infants and the baptism of adults were used, with the latter being more common. During the fourth century, a time when a very severe approach to the sacrament of penance was taken, it was not unusual for children of Christian parents not to be baptized until they were adults. After the Christianization of the Roman Empire, infant baptism became the established practice within the Catholic community and remains such today.

Evidence shows too that baptism in the early centuries was administered both by immersion and by pouring of water. This was true for adults and for children. Gradually, though, in the Catholic community the practice of baptism by the pouring of water became the more common practice. By the

74

eleventh century baptism by immersion for adults was more the exception, though St. Thomas (thirteenth century) tells us that baptism of immersion for infants was still common then. Today most Catholic baptisms are via the pouring of the water, though immersion may be practiced in some parishes.

In regard to baptism, we should not overlook the catechumenate, or that process of becoming a Christian. In the early Church this was a long and demanding affair that could take several years. It was continued even after baptism in order to educate the new members fully in the ways of the community. After the Roman Empire became Christian, this period of preparation was shortened, but it still is a necessary time during which the individual can be properly instructed in the Catholic faith and given ample opportunities to live that faith. It is to be noted that in the case of infant baptism, both in the early Church and today, the entire period of the catechumenate takes place after baptism. It is the responsibility of the community to help educate and rear this child as a true Christian.

Water

Water is a tremendous symbol both of life and of destruction. Positively viewed it leads to life, and in Scripture to a "new" life. In the Old Testament flood waters came to destroy sinful man, but those in the ark were saved. They were not to continue to live the old life, but a new life pleasing to the Lord of the covenant. The Jews were led through the Red Sea and then through the River Jordan. In both instances they were leaving one way of living and committing themselves to a more faithful existence as the "people of Yahweh." John the Baptist preached a baptism of repentance. In Old Testament times a baptism of water was used to indicate a change of life—a dying to the old way and a pledge to live the new life of commitment to the Lord.

One of the themes of John's Gospel is the fact that Jesus Christ is the new life which is given to us sacramentally through baptism and the Eucharist. Note John's frequent use of the word "life" and of water episodes, ending with water and blood coming from the side of Christ. The baptism of water used by the Christian communities is their way of symbolizing and actually participating in the death-resurrection of Christ so that we all come alive in him.

Redemption

Man is a sinner. He cannot redeem himself. He needs help so that he can pass to a new life—to raise himself up and commit himself to a new way of living. The Genesis account of man's early existence showed that he could not live this new life without God's help. After the flood God called Abraham and the whole history of salvation begins, climaxing in Jesus Christ. Jesus taught us how to live; he lived this way, and he sealed it with a full commitment of his life, for he knew it was a "radical" way of living. He died and rose again. Our redemption comes through Jesus Christ. We need to enter into this mystery of Christ, into his death and resurrection. The fullness of man's living is not a this-life-only existence. Only the fullness of life in Christ, begun in this life and continued in what lies after our death, pictures what life can be for the human race. If you read the epistles of Paul, this notion of our entering into the death-resurrection mystery of Christ comes up again and again as descriptive of what the Christian life is all about.

Community

In order for Christ's work to continue, in order to give all people a way of entering into this mystery, and in order that he could be with us and help us, Jesus Christ founded a faith community—the Church. Baptism is our way of entering into this community, a kind of initiation rite. We die and rise with Christ. The rite of baptism through immersion in the water illustrates this beautifully. We die but then we rise. The baptismal waters give us new life. The community commits itself to the lifelong struggle of making Christ's redemption happen to the world so that all of creation belongs to Christ.

All the members of this community commit themselves to this same struggle. Today we do not always see this struggle sharply. In the early centuries, becoming a Christian was a commitment to live a life radically different from that of your contemporaries. When the Western world became Christian, Christians became much like their neighbors. Too often this led to a lessening of the real living of a commitment. Today we are still being invited to participate in this commitment and in this struggle. The world today is far from being Christian to the core. We are free to accept the invitation or to reject it.

Baptism and the catechumenate are community affairs. It is the community which accepts this new member into its midst. This community should be present when this takes place in order to welcome the new member and to pledge the community's support. It is the community's task to see to it that this new member is reared as a Christian. The community not only educates, but it also pledges itself to create that atmosphere of love, peace, justice, and righteousness so that the new Christians breathe in a Christian atmosphere and are helped by their surroundings.

Infant Baptism

Infant baptism is the common practice in the Catholic Church today. In the early centuries adult baptism was the common practice, and the slow process through the catechumenate allowed the person to become more acquainted with the commitment to be made and gave the community ample time to evaluate the prospective member. Today we are baptized and then have to be educated, formed, helped to come to that moment when we realize what the commitment is, and then make our own decision to ratify it or go away. Only with this ratification do we become full, committed members of the community.

Infant baptism has its good points. It does manifest the fact that our salvation comes from God's mercy and not from our actions. It shows the community its responsibility regarding the faith-education of the children. For those who believe in grace, in the spiritual life of the people of God, it shows how the infants are being brought into the community so that they can be reared in the tender, loving care of this community's life of grace. The children's responsibility arises when they grow and are able to make their own commitment. For all of us a special kind of commitment is faced as we grow into adulthood and have to give birth to our adult faith.

Rite of Baptism

The way a community celebrates baptism is very important. More than a handful of persons should be present. Celebrating this sacrament during a Sunday Mass is a wonderful setting. Having special "baptism Masses" at other than scheduled times is also helpful.

The revised rite for infant baptism includes the following:

1. Greeting of the parents, child and godparents.
2. Scriptural reading and brief homily.
3. Prayer of the faithful.
4. Prayer of exorcism and anointing on the breast.
5. Blessing of the water (if necessary).
6. Baptismal promises and profession of faith.
7. Baptism, plus the anointing with chrism, clothing with a white garment, and the presentation of a candle.

8. Conclusion: Our Father and blessings of mother, father, and all present.

The revised rite for adult baptism in its simple form is much the same; however, it usually includes the reception of confirmation and of the Holy Eucharist. This simple rite is the one more commonly used in the U.S.A. In some countries, especially missionary countries, the full rite is used and includes three stages which take place over an extended period of time.

• Rite of Becoming Catechumens
This includes a first instruction, a promise to continue to study under Christ's leadership, the renunciation of non-Christian worship, and the giving of a new name. There is a celebration of the word of God which includes the giving of a copy of the Gospels to the catechumens.

During the course of the following months (or even years) the catechumens are instructed in the teachings of the Church and led to a living of the Christian way of life and worship. During the course of this time there are a number of celebrations of the word of God which would include special prayers and exorcisms as well as blessings of the catechumens.

• Rite of Election
Around the beginning of Lent those catechumens judged ready are presented for admission into the final stages of preparation for baptism. Their names are solemnly enrolled as ones preparing for baptism on Holy Saturday. On the third, fourth and fifth Sundays of Lent the scrutinies take place. These are basically small ceremonies during the first part of the Mass at which time special prayers, blessings, and exorcisms occur. It should be noted that just as in the early days of the Church the catechumens (now called the elect) are ordinarily dismissed at this time and the Eucharist is celebrated after they leave. There are also two ceremonies of presentation at which

time the elect are entrusted with the two Church documents (the Creed and the Lord's Prayer) which summarize the Church's teachings and its way of prayer.

• Rite of Sacraments of Initiation

The sacraments of baptism and of confirmation are received during the Holy Saturday vigil service. The rite of baptism includes a special litany, blessing of the water, baptismal promises and profession of faith, and baptism itself, including clothing with the white garment and presentation of a lighted candle. Immediately following, the sacrament of confirmation is administered in the simple rite of prayer, imposition of hands on the head of the newly baptized and the anointing with chrism. The eucharistic celebration continues and the newly baptized receive Communion for the first time.

Confirmation

During the Vigil Service on Holy Saturday night, adult catechumens are received into full membership in the Catholic community via the reception of three sacraments: baptism, confirmation, and the Eucharist. It is only when we are able to participate fully in the activities of the community and especially in the worship life that we are full members; hence the three sacraments. This is what happened in the early Church and is still maintained in the Eastern rites of the Catholic Church. All three sacraments are administered even to babies. In some Spanish-speaking segments of the Latin rite, both baptism and confirmation are administered to infants. Most of us in the Latin rite, though, received confirmation in grade school.

Two interrelated questions are discussed today: Just what is confirmation, and when should it be received?

What is confirmation? Are there two sacraments of initiation? What is the difference? Confirmation has always been looked upon as a sacrament of Christian adulthood, a sacrament of Catholic Action, a sacrament of a mature Christian. When we are grown we have a special sharing in the mission of the Church. Infants and children are a part of the community, and in their own way they help a community to grow and to bear witness to the Christian message. However, "mature" Catholics are expected to do this in a special way. They are old enough to know who and what they are; they are expected to measure up to all the challenges of Christian living. They are not just *potential* adult members; they are *actual* adult members of the community. At baptism I become a member of the community; at confirmation I officially take upon myself all the responsibilities of the Christian adult.

Because of this note of maturation, there has been much discussion today as to when this sacrament should be received. All solutions seem to have their merits. Confirmation, administered at baptism, bears testimony to what I am going to be and gives me all the help I shall need to measure up as I grow up. Confirmation at First Communion time shows that, although I am not yet fully grown, I am old enough to share in the eucharistic meal and in the mission of the Church. Confirmation at adolescence comes at a time of trial and special challenge. I need the help of this sacrament to handle the challenges of this age. Confirmation received when I am a young adult bears witness to the fact that I am now a full-grown member of this community and am pledging myself to full acceptance of this community and all that it stands for.

The experience of "born again" Christians and of charismatics (baptism of the Spirit) point to the fullness of the adult witness to Christ's message, to the graces of the Holy Spirit, and to the impact of the Spirit upon adults with open minds and hearts. Although some charismatics can be a little far out in their reading of the Spirit, most of them testify in a wonderful way to the kind of life that an adult Catholic, confirmed in the Spirit, ought to live. It is not easy to live the fullness of Christ's message in the dog-eat-dog world in which we live.

Catholics today, like the Christians of the early centuries living in a pagan world, must still work at it. The grace of the Spirit is there to help us.

DISCUSSION QUESTIONS

1. What role does the community play in baptism? In confirmation? Why is this important?
2. Is it too easy to become a Catholic?
3. Does infant baptism force the Catholic faith upon a child who is too young to understand its significance?
4. How will you know when you are ready to accept or reject your baptismal vows?
5. If adult baptism were the practice rather than infant baptism, would the Church community have better members?
6. Should education in one's faith come before or after baptism?
7. Does one need to be baptized to be an official member of the Church? Why?
8. When should confirmation be received? Why?

READINGS

Antekeier, Charles and Janet and Van Vandagriff. *Confirmation: The Power of the Spirit.* Ave Maria, 1972.

Haas, La Verne. *Personal Pentecost.* Abbey Press, 1973.

Hellwig, Monika. *The Meaning of the Sacraments.* Pflaum, 1972. Chapters 1 and 2.

O'Shea, William. *Sacraments of Initiation.* Prentice-Hall, 1966.

Richards, Hubert and Peter De Rosa. *Christ in Our World.* Bruce, 1966. Chapters II and III.

11 HEALING AND RECONCILIATION

Anyone who reads the Gospels, even in a cursory way, will note that there is mention of sin and of Christ's handling of it. There is the woman taken in adultery (Jn 8:1–11), the prodigal son (Lk 15:1–24), the cure of the paralytic (Lk 5:18–26), the pardoning of the sinful woman (Lk 7:36–50), the promise made to Peter (Mt 16:19), and on Easter night the giving of the power to forgive sins (Jn 20:19–23). Sin and forgiveness of sin are there in the Gospels.

History

A study of the development of the sacrament of penance in the Catholic Church is an excellent example of the growth and development syndrome that was discussed in Chapter 1. A certain pattern is there. The Church community felt the need for reconciliation, and a certain rite was developed based upon the current understanding of sin. As time passed a new need arose and the rite was changed. There are many ways of presenting the history of this sacrament within the Catholic community. Because of the emphasis that was placed on the following points in the respective periods, we can sum up this history in these three words: (1) penance or satisfaction, (2) confession, and (3) reconciliation.

1. *Satisfaction:* In the early centuries, Christians were expected to live a strong Christian life. They were to be living witnesses to the redemptive life of Christ, to what the Church was all about. Every failure to be such a witness called for penance. By the fourth century a rather severe approach had evolved in the so-called "canonical discipline." This included the confession of certain major sins (murder, adultery, apostasy) to the bishop. A severe penance was imposed and carried out; only after that would the reconciliation ceremony take place. It was allowed only once in one's life, although it could also be received on one's deathbed. If this seems harsh, keep in mind that the Church and its members were to be living witnesses to this mission of holiness, of manifesting the Christ-life to the world. Those who again failed publicly were not received back into the full membership of the community. They were not looked upon as good witnesses.

2. *Confession:* From the fifth century on, an attitude of mercy developed and the sacrament was received more than once. Later, confession of devotion (which did not involve serious sin) was practiced. It was found that a manifestation of one's state of conscience could be a great help to one seeking to become a better Christian. It was only around the year 1000 that absolution was given before the penance was performed. In 1215 annual confession was prescribed, but this was obligatory only for those who needed to be reconciled with the community, so that they could partake of the Lord's supper. The Council of Trent (1551) presented the basic Catholic teaching: Confession is a sacrament involving acts of the penitent (examination of conscience, sorrow, confession, amendment, penance) and of the confessor (absolution). In 1614 the ritual called for the screen between the confessor and the penitent.

Up until the 1960's "good" Catholics went to confession at least once a month. They did so anonymously, but a regular confessor was suggested. Emphasis was placed on integral confessions (exact numbers and kinds). Problems developed with this type of confession. They were too impersonal and became routine affairs. Penitents were reciting "grocery lists" rather than manifesting their state of conscience.

3. *Reconciliation:* In recent decades efforts have been made to make confession a personal encounter with Christ and thus more profitable. This has led to the new rite, with its face-to-face option, with its emphasis on a person's state of being rather than a "grocery list," and with its more personal penances. It is a reconciliation, a healing. I need to know what I have done and why, as well as what I am going to do about it. I pledge that I will do this. I am reconciled by means of the absolution given by the appointed minister. It is in truth a celebration.

The new rite has the following elements:

- Welcoming the penitent.
- Reading the word of God (optional). (This may take place before the individual goes into the confessional.)
- Confession of sins, which is a manifestation of conscience rather than a listing and may include some "counseling discussion" in order to see what should be done, and will lead to the imposing of some personal act of penance or satisfaction.
- Prayer of the penitent asking for forgiveness; the granting of absolution.
- Proclamation of praise and dismissal of the penitent.

Sin—Exclusion—Reconciliation

Three ideas which are basic to the proper understanding of this sacrament are: (1) sin, (2) exclusion, and (3) reconciliation. We need to grasp these ideas in their fullness and in their interrelation in order to appreciate the sacrament.

1. *Sin:* Sin has commonly been defined as any thought, word or deed contrary to the law of God. This is a neat, compact definition but it does not give us a deep, personal sense of what sin is all about. Such a sense should come from a fuller understanding of sin and its relationship to self, to community and to God. As a self, I am a unique person, to be accepted and appreciated for what I am. I am an individual who can respond to personal challenges directed my way. Only I can make myself be "me." The community is a group to which I belong, to which I commit myself, and from which I accept responsibilities. Whatever I do (twenty-four hours a day), I represent this community. I am to be a living witness to that holiness for which it stands. God invites me to enter into a most intimate personal love relationship with himself and awaits my response.

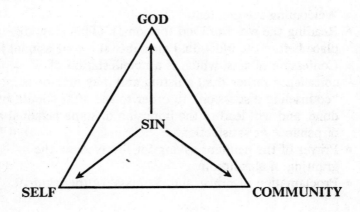

Sin has a threefold dimension. I am not doing what I pledged I would do for myself, for my community, for my God. I am not living up to what I truly am or can be as a person. I have committed myself to this community and its ideals, its goals, its standards, its mission. I am not living up to this commitment; I am not contributing to this community in a positive way; I am even polluting it. Finally, I am not, with the totality of my being, responding to a loving God who offers me himself. I am not using all my talents to love him in return.

Much of my appreciation for what is "sinful" or not will depend upon my basic approach to Christian living. Some follow a "do and don't" system. This is a legal, juridical approach that strives toward minimal morality at best. I get by. Little sins can be looked upon as all right, just as long as I avoid the big ones. If I am motivated by love, I ask the question: What else can I do? rather than Do I have to? God loves me, and I want to respond with the fullness of my being. I want to love myself, my neighbor, and my God—a triangle of love relationships. If I strive after an ideal in moral living, I want to use all my talents in the best possible way. I am never content with just getting by, but want to do all I am capable of doing. I measure up to the limits of my potential. This last approach does demand personal maturation. I must know myself and my responsibilities. I must have control over myself so that I am able to respond fully with all my talents to the challenges that come my way.

In all this I never forget that I am a sinner. Though we are all basically good, we do need to realize our mistakes, our failures, our refusals. Too often we overlook the fact that we are sinners, that we need to grow, to improve. Sin is the failure to measure up to all that I am and can be in relationship to self/community/God.

2. *Exclusion:* Violations of a community's standards can gradually harm my relationship with that community. They will weaken the bond that unites us, and if repeated too often they will lead to an estrangement, and possibly even to exclusion. Serious violations mean that I am not being a worthy witness to what this community stands for. I am not, in a serious way, living up to what this community has every right to expect from me. My presence is doing harm rather than good.

I am more than failing to do my part. I am not that living witness to holiness that can be expected from every member of this community, even if perfect holiness is not expected. For instance, a misbehaving child is sent from the room or from the dinner table, a student is suspended from school, a driver's license is suspended, a person is excommunicated from the Church community, and a serious mortal sin removes my good standing in the community.

3. *Reconciliation:* For all such cases, reconciliation is necessary. "Mom, I'm sorry. I learned my lesson." Reconciliation is a process of healing. It does involve a conversion, a recommitment. I recognize that I was wrong; I am sorry; I know what I have to do; I pledge myself to do it. Since we are all sinners, this is a constant occurrence in our lives. However, only in cases of real exclusion from the community must it be done in a public way. Properly done, it is a celebration, like the feast when the prodigal son returned home.

Reconciliation is necessary. A child must apologize and tell his mother that he learned his lesson. A student must seek reinstatement in the school community. In a faith community it is necessary in varying degrees. We need some kind of reconciliation every time we hurt those we love (kiss and make up). Only when we have broken from the community and have been excluded from full participation in its services and celebrations is sacramental reconciliation required. In the Catholic Church the sacraments of baptism and reconciliation are the official rites for such reconciliation. Baptism brought me from non-life to life in this community. The sacrament of penance (confession, reconciliation) takes place after I have been excluded from the community for serious failures in measuring up to being a living witness to Christ. I need an official reconciliation with the community. I can become myself by acknowledging my guilt to myself and by pledging future improvement. In order to make this acknowledgement and pledge to the community, I need to seek out the individual members or make use of the official ritual provided by the community for such reconciliation.

Some Questions

1. Is sacramental penance necessary? The sacrament *must* be received only when there has been serious exclusion from the community (traditionally called "mortal" sin). Even annual confession is required only when this exclusion has taken place. Otherwise, it is never necessary to receive this sacrament. It could be that many of the arguments against receiving it (I prefer to tell my sins to God; I get more out of going to the person I hurt and telling him I am sorry, etc.) point out the need to come up with a deeper insight into what sin is all about and its effect upon the community. Perhaps there are smaller failings that hurt the community as well as greater sins that exclude from the community. Those who operate out of love or out of an ideal morality are never satisfied with a minimal response. There is no need to be concerned that they will not do all they should for self, for the community and for God.

2. Is confession worth it? People who make proper use of the sacrament find it very helpful. It demands that I see myself for what I really am. Am I living up to my commitments? What kind of Christian have I been? It leads to a deeper realization of my faults, of God's forgiveness, of the social dimension of sin, and then to a stronger commitment to my Christian ideals. I will get out of it what I put into it. Further, as we struggle to become fuller witnesses to Christ, we at times have problems and want to get some advice on what to do about them. Going to confession to a priest provides for that. In addition, the sacraments give grace. This sacrament focuses the healing power of God on our needs and obtains the sup-

port of the community in our work to become better Christians. Thus, the question of how often should a person go to confession might be answered: "As often as I can do so meaningfully."

3. When should a child's First Confession take place? When most of us were in the first grade, it was the practice to have every child go to confession before receiving Holy Communion. In recent years, this practice has been seriously questioned. No one should ever be forced to receive this sacrament, and many youngsters may not be able to receive it profitably. Current practice has been to catechize the child for confession before First Communion. Confession is to be made available for those who wish to receive the sacrament, but no one is forced to go. Many think it is better to have children participate in various penance services during the first years of grade school and then gradually lead them to the sacrament in the middle grades. This is basically an individual and personal question. The answer will vary from child to child.

DISCUSSION QUESTIONS

1. Has today's generation been brought up to fear sin less than other generations? Whatever happened to the concept of sin?

2. Discuss the things that you were taught about sin when you were very young. How have your views changed?

3. What do you think of the conditions under which you received this sacrament for the first time? What would you advise for children today?

4. Explain why sin is a community illness.

5. Discuss whether confession today is too easy on the penitent, encouraging mediocrity rather than challenging to greatness.

6. Write out sample confessions of the 1950's and of today.

READINGS

Bassett, Bernard. *Guilty, O Lord.* Doubleday, 1975.

Foley, Leonard. *What's Happening to Confession?* St. Anthony Messenger, 1970.

Jeep, Elizabeth McMahon. *Implementing the Rite.* Liturgical Conference, 1976.

Kiefer, Ralph and Frederick McManus. *Understanding the Document.* Liturgical Conference, 1975.

Mitchell, Nathan, ed. *Background and Directions.* Liturgical Conference, 1978.

Orsy, Ladislas. *The Evolving Church and the Sacrament of Penance.* Dimension Books, 1978.

Shea, John. *What a Modern Catholic Believes About Sin.* Thomas More, 1971.

12 NOURISHMENT AND WORSHIP: THE EUCHARIST

The three Synoptic evangelists and Paul recall for us how Jesus, at the Last Supper, took bread, blessed it, broke it, and shared it with his apostles. He also took the cup of wine, blessed it, and shared it (Mt 26:26–28; Mk 14:22–24; Lk 22: 19–20; 1 Cor 11:23–26). Chapter 6 of John's Gospel contains the magnificent bread of life discourse which gives us background on how to understand this eucharistic meal of Christ. It was this Last Supper meal which the apostles and the early Christians gathered together to celebrate in memory of him. Although they continued to attend prayer services in the temple and the synagogue, these first Christians gathered on Sundays (the day of Christ's resurrection) for a fraternal meal and the celebration of the Eucharist. Around 160, the two parts (the prayer service and the Eucharist) were fused together, and in the fourth century Latin replaced Greek as the language in which the liturgy was celebrated. The Mass, as it existed in the second century, was very much like the Mass of today.

If you look at the development of the Mass over the centuries, you will note that there have been changes. For the most part these have followed a kind of cycle, and today we are moving back more and more toward the practices of the

	Second Century	Today
TEACHING PART	readings homily common prayer kiss of peace	introductory rites (greeting, penitential, praise, prayer) readings homily (creed) prayer of the faithful
SACRIFICIAL PART	presentation of bread and wine prayer of thanksgiving breaking of bread Communion—both species collection for poor	offertory or presentation of gifts eucharistic prayer of thanks kiss of peace Communion concluding prayers and blessing

early Church. Those earlier expressions were good ones, simple and meaningful. Here are a few examples:

- The altar in the early centuries was a simple table, often carried in for the service. The priest faced the people. By the year 1000, the altar had become rather ornate and been moved up against the wall of the church, and the priest had his back to the people. Today the altar has again become a table with the priest facing the people.

- In the early Church everyone participated fully in the liturgy. In the Middle Ages this diminished and reached a very low ebb in the nineteenth century. Today there is again a movement toward the fullest possible participation on the part of all.

- In the early Church there was an offertory procession in which gifts were brought forward for use in the Mass itself and for giving to the poor. Later this died out as the Mass became the action of the priest alone. Today, in addition to the offertory collection, there is often a small, symbolic offertory procession.

• In the first centuries the entire Mass was prayed aloud. Starting in the seventh century the canon of the Mass was recited quietly by the priest. Today the entire Mass is again prayed aloud.

• The early Christians received Communion every time they celebrated the Mass. From the fifth century on this practice declined. In 1215 the Fourth Lateran Council decreed that all Catholics should receive Communion at least once a year. From then until today there have been movements (and counter-movements) toward more frequent reception of Communion. In 1905 Pius X issued his decree on frequent Communion which led to daily Communion, and in 1910 his decree on First Communion lowered the age for First Communion from around 13 to 7 or 8.

• During the first three centuries there was no eucharistic fast. In the fourth century the fast became universal, with no food or drink from midnight on. Decrees in 1953, 1957, and 1964 gradually changed this to our present regulations of abstaining for one hour from food or drink, with water and medicine permitted at any time.

• In the early Church, Communion was received in the hand, and under both species. In the ninth century Communion was received on the tongue, and in the twelfth century the cup for the laity disappeared. Today Communion is received under both species at times, and is permitted in the hand in over forty countries.

Understanding the Mass

Despite the fact that the Mass, the celebration of the Eucharist, is the central core around which everything revolves and toward which everything is directed, it is often not properly understood. It is the Eucharist that creates the Christ community. We come together to do this in memory of him, to remember him. (To remember means "to make present".) We celebrate his presence and become one with him and with each other in common cause and fellowship.

The Eucharist is the central and most important sacrament. All of the others are geared toward participation in the Eucharist, the full mystery of Christ. The Mass is a carrying on of the work of salvation effected by Christ. It is a celebration of the entire mystery of Christ: his life, mission, suffering, resurrection, etc. It is a celebration of the real meaning of the Christian life, revealing what life means as a result of the coming of Christ, and what our life means as illustrated by Christ. It is a celebration of our baptism and of our union with Christ in heaven. All this is being celebrated and made present now. This is the priestly work of Christ.

We gather together as a family, as a community, as a tightly-knit group with common beliefs, a common tradition, common goals. We come together to celebrate events and mysteries meaningful to the entire group. It is a "we" thing which demands the total giving of all of us to make it go. The Catholic Church today is celebrating the Christ-event in a liturgical manner.

Jesus gave us a meal setting. The symbolic sharing of bread and wine in a community meal manifests our togetherness, our commitments to a common cause, our giving, sharing, and receiving together. The Mass is likewise a sacrifice, tied in with Calvary. Christ gave himself in total oblation. We Christians are likewise called upon to give of ourselves to the cause of Christ.

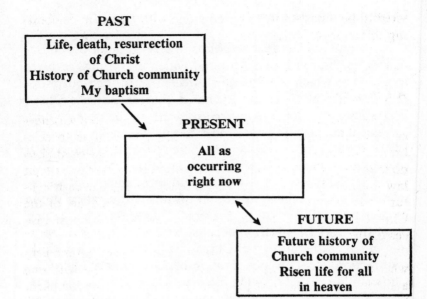

When celebrating liturgy we transcend our regular time concepts. We use what may be called liturgical time. This enables us to make the past and the future present *now*. The Jewish people celebrate their Passover in which they make present *now* what happened at the first exodus—their deliverance. In the Mass we celebrate the total mystery of Christ and salvation—the entire life of Christ, our own baptism (our first encounter with Christ), and our future resurrection in heaven (our lasting encounter with Christ). The Mass is a liturgical celebration of what *was* (Christ, Christian tradition), what *is* (Church today), and what *will be* (heaven).

Thus, to celebrate the Eucharist with Christ and with my brothers and sisters in Christ is not an obligation; it is a tremendous privilege. I am present at and participating in this whole mystery of life and love. I am not a spectator; I am invited to be a part of it, to become one with Christ in celebrating this liturgy.

A Few Questions

1. *Sunday Obligation?* In the early Church there was never a question of Sunday obligation. Christians came to celebrate the Eucharist as a privilege, something they wanted to do and were glad to be a part of. The first record of an explicit law on Sunday observance came in 506. In the eleventh century, the Decree of Gratian made this a universal law of the Church. Today this Sunday observance begins in most dioceses with Saturday evening Masses.

2. *Intercommunion?* In the current era of ecumenism where all churches are open to one another, sharing with one another, and cooperating with one another, the question of intercommunion arises. Why not share in the Lord's supper even if you are not a member of this particular faith community? At times this is done, but not always with official sanction. On rare occasions it is permitted in the Catholic Church. Some Protestant Churches welcome anyone who has been baptized; some allow only their own members to receive at their services. It is not an easy question to answer. The Eucharist is viewed both as a sign of unity and as a cause of unity. Why not receive together and help our unity to grow? On the other hand, receiving together implies an acceptance of and a commitment to all that this community stands for. This needs to be resolved before any official sanction of regular intercommunion will take place in the Catholic Church.

3. *Real Presence?* Some Christian Churches say that Christ is present only in faith; others affirm his presence in the act of communicating. The Catholic Church holds for the real presence of Jesus in the Eucharist. But how is Jesus present?

He is not present physically in the same way that this book is present to you or the way that a teacher and a class are together in a room. He is not just present there by his power or by his authority as a government authority might be. His presence is not just evoked by the presence of a picture or a memento. In Catholic tradition, Christ is really but sacramentally present to the believer. The sacrament, in its symbol and in its ritual, makes present here and now the saving reality of Christ that it symbolizes. This is true of all the sacraments. In the sacrificial meal of the Eucharist, it is Christ himself who is made present and presented to us as the food and drink that enables us to partake fully of the fruits of his sacrifice.

DISCUSSION QUESTIONS

1. Discuss attendance at weekly Mass as a privilege and as an obligation. Which is it for you?
2. Is it necessary to understand what is meant by community in order to understand the Eucharist? What is the relationship between the two?
3. How should people be prepared for reception of the Eucharist?
4. What is the significance of the eucharistic fast? Should it be more greatly emphasized?
5. Do you think that the Eucharist should be received for the first time in a class or alone with family and friends? Why?
6. What kinds of changes do you think should be made in the celebration of the Mass?

READINGS

Champlin, Joseph. *The New Yet Old Mass.* Ave Maria, 1977.
Guzie, Tad. *Jesus and the Eucharist.* Paulist, 1974.

McGloin, Joseph. *How To Get More Out of the Mass.* Liguori, 1974.
Padavano, Anthony. *Presence and Structure.* Paulist, 1976.
Powers, Joseph. *Eucharistic Theology.* Herder and Herder, 1967.

13 STATES OF LIFE: MINISTRY IN THE CHURCH

History

Jesus Christ is the priest in the Catholic tradition. He possessed the fullness of the priesthood, and all Christians, ordained or not, share in this one full priesthood of Christ. What did Christ's priesthood entail? What was its purpose? What was his ministry? As mentioned in the section on the Church, Christ took upon himself human nature in order to make us "whole." Christ gave of himself totally, even unto death on the cross. Throughout his life he taught people; he comforted them; he fed them; he was concerned about their total well-being. His ministry was not just to teach and not just to lead in worship. It was to serve the whole person.

This is the ministry that developed in the Church, though not all was done by the apostles. Very early in the history of the Church, deacons and deaconesses appeared and were entrusted with many tasks (taking care of the poor, administering baptism, taking Communion to the sick) so that the apostles and their successors were free to teach and to preside at the Eucharist. As the Church grew, the ministry to the whole person grew as well, although the various works of the ministry were shared by the clergy, the religious, and the laity. The tremendous growth in religious over the centuries enabled the Church to minister effectively to the spiritual and bodily needs of the people of the world even down to the present day. The role of the laity during these latter centuries seemed to diminish.

In recent decades the role of the laity is again being recognized and championed. The roles of the priest and of the religious have both undergone serious examination. Many have left the priesthood and the religious life. Currently, as the concepts of the Church and of the roles as priest, religious and laity are being more clearly understood and delineated, the picture seems to be stabilizing itself.

Ministry in the Church

The Church is composed of a variety of members, all of whom share in the one priesthood of Christ insofar as they offer themselves, participate in his mission, and live to the fullest his message today and help it to be lived by others. In the Roman Catholic tradition the sacraments of baptism and confirmation initiate a person fully into this general priesthood. Lay members of the Church community exercise this ministry through membership in the parish council and through various committee and personal assignments made by the community. In addition some individuals can serve in a special way as members of a parish "team": the director of music, the religious education director, the youth minister, the principal of the school, etc.

In addition, the sacrament of holy orders designates and consecrates one to a leadership role in the Church. This ordained leadership performs a service of authority in that it establishes, maintains, and fosters order and unity within the community. This leadership performs a service of ministry (1) in word (teaching, preaching the Gospel), (2) in worship (being a leader at the Eucharist, administering the sacraments), (3) in personally witnessing to the Gospel (being holy), and (4) in actions in the "world" that serve to bring Christ into all of creation.

For the most part these ordained leaders have been the bishops and the priests. In recent years the Church has re-established the state of permanent deacons. Most of these are married men who are given the proper formation and education and then assigned to a parish. They remain married; they retain their regular job in life; they take over some of the tasks of the priests so that the total work of the parish can go forward. They are able to perform all the duties of a deacon: distribute Communion, perform marriages, instruct people in the faith, preach, preside at funerals, baptize, etc.

In a similar vein, some dioceses in very recent years have begun a lay pastoral ministry program. These programs prepare dedicated men and women who wish to dedicate themselves more fully to working in the ministry of the Church. After they complete the program, they are expected to devote some years of their lives to the active ministry in the diocese in collaboration with other ministers, clerical and lay.

Finally, it does seem proper to mention the religious. These are men and women who take upon themselves the vows of poverty, chastity and obedience. They belong to an organized society which dedicates itself to various works of the Church's ministry. Because of the total availability of these religious many works of the ministry go on that perhaps might not otherwise have been possible.

In all of the above, this ministry is not a personal gift held by a solitary individual, but is one's share in a collegial responsibility held by the group. This is especially true for those who by ordination are incorporated into the group of "ordained leaders." This ordination designates and consecrates them to a leadership role in the Church; it sanctifies them by giving strength to live a life of dedicated service to the Church community.

The Priest

The priest's primary role is to serve the community. He does this as a pastor—an organizer, coordinator, leader, one who forms this small group of people into a community of God's people. He is also a teacher and a preacher. He preaches to those who need to be evangelized; he teaches those who need to be educated (which comes after evangelization). He is a counselor to those with ordinary human problems as well as with spiritual ones. He is a sanctifier by celebrating the Eucharist, by administering the sacraments, and by personal example.

A priest, like all the rest of us, is still a human being. He is not always perfect, nor does every one possess all of the following qualities that it is generally felt a priest should have: he should be human, understanding, dedicated, strong, a man of God, a man of faith, prayerful, and approachable; he must be a leader who is also not only knowledgeable but growing in knowledge.

Today everyone seems to get evaluated in one way or another. Basic criteria for evaluating the work of a parish priest would include his availability, the way he is used or not used by the community, the worship life, the apostolic life and theological alertness of the community, and the development of the community in understanding the Catholic faith in all its fullness.

To be able to measure up to these high ideals a priest needs to be formed in his own personal prayer life, in the teachings of the community, in leading liturgy, in preaching, and in how to work with people. This formation is done during his seminary training, which includes ecumenical and university settings, as well as during a period of apprenticeship in a parish faith community. Today the seminary involves four years of education and formation after one has completed his university studies. Academically the seminarian pursues studies in such areas as Scripture, Church doctrine, morality, Church history, Church law, psychology, Church administration, preaching, and liturgy. He is given formation in his own personal prayer life, which is so important for him as a priest ministering to the needs of a community. As he goes through the seminary he is given practical experiences in liturgy, in preaching, etc. During his year as a deacon he is assigned to some parish in the diocese for an intensive apprenticeship into the life of a parish priest.

Celibacy

One of the much discussed questions about priesthood in recent decades has been that of celibacy. Celibacy was not always a rule in the Catholic Church, and it was not required by Christ. St. Peter was married. However, from the fourth century on the Church has struggled to make it the rule, and a lived rule. In the twelfth century it became obligatory for the Latin rite clergy, although not all have practiced it faithfully. Today this rule has been strongly challenged. Some say this is one of the main reasons why so many priests have left the priesthood and why so few are entering the seminary. Others deny this. Many are pushing for optional celibacy. Pope John Paul II in 1979 took a strong position in favor of celibacy as a requirement for the Latin rite clergy.

Celibacy is not an essential part of the priesthood. It is a Church requirement that can be changed. It must be recalled, however, that any Church community has the power within itself to set up certain requirements for certain offices or functions. Thus, this rule is not out of line with what can be done in a community.

Celibacy is not always understood, even by celibates themselves. It is not a choice between God and a woman; it is not a choice between a natural value (marriage) and a supernatural value (the kingdom of God). Both values are good in themselves. It does so happen at times, because of my total commitment to a certain work (for instance, as a research scientist), that I have no other choice than to choose celibacy. If I want to devote myself in this way to this work, then I cannot take upon myself the responsibility of marriage. This reason is very basic to understanding celibacy which is chosen for the sake of Christ and the kingdom of God. I totally commit myself to the work of this kingdom and make myself totally available to it. Edward Schillebeeckx, in his book *Celibacy,* gives an excellent treatise on this.

Further, celibacy does bear witness to the life of faith, to the life of grace, to the future resurrected life with God, and to holiness (even though the priest himself is not a saint). That state of life (celibacy) does witness to all these things and makes people aware of them. Many people would regret the fact of not having a celibate clergy. This witness value is important. (Note that this would not rule out optional celibacy.)

Women in the Ministry

A question that is being asked more and more frequently these days is: Should women be ordained into the Catholic priesthood? Many Catholics, both men and women, lay and religious, feel that they should. The official Church position, strongly reiterated by Pope Paul VI and Pope John Paul II, is that they should not be ordained. The following are some of the reasons advanced against the ordination of women.

- Although Jesus challenged many of the customs of his day, he did not call women to be among his twelve disciples. This is indicative of the fact that Jesus did not want women to function in a priestly capacity.

- The ordained priest acts officially in the person of Christ when celebrating the Mass. Only a male priest can represent Christ, who was a male.
- The apostles did not choose women either to fill the place of Judas or to act in a priestly capacity. There is no evidence that any women were ordained in the apostolic Church.
- Mary was not called to be an apostle, nor did she fulfill a priestly function in the early Church, yet no one could equal her sanctity and perfection. Thus, obviously, it is not the will of God that women be ordained.
- Women are complementary to men. Both fulfill different functions in life.
- It is the long tradition of the Catholic Church not to ordain women.
- Ordination is not a right; it is a special call from God. No one has the right to be ordained.

Those who favor ordination for women also have a list of arguments for their position.

- It is unjust to exclude women from this office simply because of their sex without regard to personal qualifications.
- Through baptism all participate in the priesthood of the faithful. All likewise should be eligible to test their vocation for pastoral office.
- Many women feel that they are called by the Holy Spirit to function in a sacramental capacity.
- Women have a special experience of life which men do not have and could thus bring special insight into the pastorate and thus into the Church.

- Many Anglican and Protestant churches favor the ordination of women to the ministry. We must seriously weigh this experience and take into consideration the theological reasons given by these churches when they made the decision to ordain women.
- Other long-standing traditions of the Church have been changed in the past twenty years. Therefore, the fact that not ordaining women is a tradition should not be allowed to bar women from the priesthood.
- Galatians 3:28 ("There does not exist among you Jew or Greek, slave or freeman, male or female. All are one in Christ Jesus") and other Scripture passages that teach the equality of men and women must be actualized.

The question of whether or not to ordain women to the priesthood is a difficult one. Polls taken in the United States show that an increasing number of Catholics favor such ordination, but a substantial number strongly oppose it. The serious discussion of this question is an on-going one. The 1979 report from the task force of the Catholic Biblical Association concludes that there is no New Testament evidence against the ordination of women and that what evidence is there, while not decisive, seems to favor their ordination.

Conclusion

The core question here is ministry; the questions of celibacy and women priests, important though they may be, are peripheral. They are not an essential element of ministry. The Church community today has to carry on the mission of Jesus Christ with all its members involved in one way or the other. Throughout history the Spirit has always raised up sufficient ministers (priests, religious, committed lay persons) to see that this work is accomplished. Each age has brought its own special challenges. The Church, guided by the Spirit, has to meet the needs of today, and this same Spirit will raise up sufficient ministers to do the job. The work of Christ will not suffer because of a lack of sufficient celibate priests.

DISCUSSION QUESTIONS

1. Which of the "roles" (teacher, preacher, sanctifier, counselor, pastor) are special to the ordained priest? Which could be carried out by members of the community?
2. Can a celibate priest identify with the problems that the families in his parish face? Would he be more effective if he were married and had a family of his own?
3. Explain why the ministry is not a personal gift held by a solitary individual.
4. What do you feel has caused the decline in priestly vocations?
5. Is God keeping people from ordaining women priests? Or are people standing in God's way?
6. How can a college student share in the priesthood of Christ?
7. Is family ministry important today? What is involved?

READINGS

Brown, Raymond. *Priest and Bishop.* Paulist, 1970.

Burghardt, Walter, ed. *Women: New Dimensions.* Paulist, 1977.

Frein, George, ed. *Celibacy.* Herder and Herder, 1968.

Gardiner, Anne Marie, ed. *Women and the Catholic Priesthood.* Paulist, 1976.

Geaney, Dennis. *Emerging Lay Ministries.* Andrews & McMeel, Inc., 1979.

Geaney, Dennis and John Ring. *What a Modern Catholic Believes About Priesthood.* Thomas More, 1971.

Schillebeeckx, Edward. *Celibacy.* Sheed and Ward, 1968.

Vatican II. *Decree on Priestly Formation, Decree on the Ministry and Life of Priests, Decree on the Renewal of Religious Life, and Decree on the Bishops' Pastoral Office in the Church.*

14 STATES OF LIFE: MARRIAGE

Established civil and indigenous marriage rituals existed when the Catholic Church came into existence. The Church accepted these as normal and valid. From the fourth century on a wedding liturgy existed in the Church, but the civil ceremony was still the recognized one. In the ninth century the civil ceremony began to take place in the church building itself and gradually became incorporated into the wedding liturgy of the Church. From the eleventh or twelfth century on the accepted marriage ritual was that of the Church. The Council of Trent in the sixteenth century laid down the basic rules, especially the necessity of a priest-witness, that are still in force today. In recent centuries, though, a Church wedding is not recognized by many nations and a civil ceremony is required. The United States recognizes both Church and civil marriages as valid.

Basic Teaching of the Church

The general Catholic teaching on marriage is as follows: God, our Creator, instituted marriage when he created the human race. Christ raised marriage to the dignity of a sacrament. The spouses are the official ministers of the sacrament since only they can give the consent that is the basis of marriage.

110

However, marriage is a public affair, and therefore a priest is required as the official witness; two other witnesses must also be present. Marriage is a vocation, a state of life. The husband and wife are prophetic witnesses to the love of Christ for his Church. In entering into the sacrament of matrimony the man and the woman are, in a way, a reincarnation of Christ's love for us. They redeem human love by incorporating it into the mystery of salvation. They witness to the mystery of Christ. They live the life of love of Christ. This is something deep, mysterious, and to be respected.

Further, just as the family is the basis of the community, so is marriage the basis of family life. Its two basic essential purposes are mutual love and children. A consummated sacramental marriage is indissoluble.

In the United States the church does not recognize the validity of civil marriages for Catholics. A marriage after a divorce is not recognized as valid by the Church. The parties no longer incur excommunication, but officially they are considered as "living in sin" and not eligible to receive the sacraments.

Mixed Marriages

Marriages between members of different faiths (Catholic and Protestant, Catholic and Jew) have never been regarded as the ideal by Catholics, by Protestants or by Jews. Today they are treated with much greater respect. If the marriage takes place in a Catholic church, a full wedding liturgy is often possible, though this does not include intercommunion. For good reasons, permission may be granted for a wedding in a Protestant church. Catholics must still affirm their commitment to their faith and state their intention of sharing this faith with their children. The non-Catholic partner is informed of this requirement but does not have to sign anything.

A mixed marriage makes great demands on both partners and can cause problems. Both may wish to share their faith with their children, and this is a legitimate aspiration. What is to be done? At times, it may mean that a couple should not get married to each other. This is an area that needs to be given very serious thought by both parties as they contemplate marriage.

Preparation for Marriage

Entering into marriage is a big step that needs proper preparation. Too often it is easier to get a marriage license than a driver's license. Making it harder to get married might prevent a great number of "mistakes." A county in Florida is thinking of introducing some kind of written test before granting a marriage license. A diocese in the northwest wants to require all young adults to see a marriage counselor before permission is granted for a wedding to take place. Pre-Cana sessions are required by most dioceses. One diocese has each engaged couple meet with a married couple for a number of sessions. Other dioceses, and certainly some parishes, have all engaged couples take a test such as the PMI (Pre-Marital Inventory). These requirements are not put there to prevent the marriage from taking place, but to help the couple to better understand themselves and the step they are about to make. It is good to know beforehand where our problem areas are so that we can see if we are able to handle them. The Church is reflecting more and more on what can be done to help people prepare themselves for the state of matrimony.

Many dioceses have regulations something like these:

- Attendance at some kind of pre-Cana series of lectures/discussions.
- Interview sessions with a priest covering such factors as family and social backgrounds, personal background,

religious attitudes, attitudes toward marriage and the
family, and reasons for desiring a religious ceremony.
- Priest interview with parents to ascertain their attitudes
toward the marriage.
- Completion of forms.
- Interview with a marriage counselor and/or the use of
the PMI.

Marriage Liturgy

Each diocese has its own specific guidelines for the wedding service, but the couple is allowed a certain amount of
freedom to construct a liturgy that is meaningful to them.

What Is Marriage?

It is easy to make laws about marriage, but it is more difficult to understand just what marriage is. Many of our current laws reflect an idea of marriage that was rather simple
and static—"a contract." Today this is not the case. In order
to know what laws and regulations should exist, especially regarding divorce and remarriage, it is crucial to have a clear understanding of what makes a marriage a marriage.

For centuries we looked upon marriage as a contract
whose object is the transfer of rights for procreative acts. The
primary end of marriage in this view is the procreation and
education of children. This is a simple, static definition of marriage which viewed consent as the central item which would
later be sealed or consummated by an act of intercourse. Marriage in this sense is easy to describe, easy to recognize, and
easy to consummate.

Today we are more and more looking upon marriage as
a covenant whose object is the formation of a community of
conjugal love naturally ordained toward the procreative process. This brings in the entire biblical background on covenants

entered into between God and man. This love relationship is characterized by fidelity, permanence, and fertility. In its fullest sense this approach to marriage might define an indissoluble marriage as one which involves this deep, total commitment to each other and to God.

Thus marriage is a state of life where two people commit themselves to growing with each other in a deep unity. This begins with a commitment, is ratified by an external ritual, and is a lifelong process of building a community of life and love.

When is such a marriage consummated so that it cannot be dissolved? Consummation can mean a state of positive permanent commitment where the two people are able to handle in a mature way all normal situations that present themselves, and most emergency ones. (No one is perfect!) If we view indissolubility less from a negative point of view (cannot be separated) and more from the positive side (be alive and live, make something of each other) we might come up with a better overall understanding of marriage. There is a lot of reflection going on in this area today.

Divorce and Remarriage

Years ago there was never any question about this in the Catholic community. The answer was no. As long as your spouse was alive, you could not marry again. No civil divorce could make this possible. Today the Church community is truly agonizing over the situation in which many couples find themselves. Should they be permitted to leave an intolerable situation and then enter into a pleasant, personally fulfilling one? Should we accept the fact that in "this" situation divorce is the correct thing to do (and allow remarriage) while at the same time working all the harder at making indissoluble marriage—the Christian ideal—realizable?

Throughout its history the Church has struggled to maintain the teachings of Christ, and it seems that the New Testament teaching is that marriage is indissoluble. Would we be unfaithful to Christ and to our Christian heritage by permitting divorce and remarriage? Or could it be that while Christ said that marriage is indissoluble, he never told us what makes a marriage a marriage? Human beings do have the natural right to get married, but these rights are never absolute. They can be restricted both by the civil community and by the faith community. There are the various impediments that prevent or hinder a marriage—age, impotency, blood relationship, previous marriage, vow of celibacy, etc. As a member of a civil community and as a member of a faith community I take upon myself the broader responsibilities that such membership entails. I am no longer a "me." I am a member of "a community," and my rights are limited by the needs and concerns of the entire community.

The Church as a pastor down through the ages has always been concerned with the needs of its people. St. Paul recognized "intolerable situations" and allowed a remarriage. This occurred in the case of two pagans, one of whom became a Christian. When the pagan partner refused to live peacefully with the Christian partner, Paul allowed the Christian partner to marry again. This principle, called the Pauline privilege, has been used often by the Church and is still used today—and often in a much broader context. Church courts today grant annulments for such reasons as psychological impotency, not just for physical impotency or lack of consent.

As the ERD process goes on, hopefully the Spirit will guide the community in the right direction. For what they are worth, we would like to share the following views. Let us theorize four possible situations:

1. Marriage was, and still is. (A happy, consummated marriage.)
2. Marriage never was. (This is what an annulment states.)

3. Marriage was, but is being dissolved. (Usually this is what a divorce means.)
4. Marriage was, but died. (What should we call this? Is it possible for a marriage to exist but then instead of growing into consummation it dies?)

In summary, the problem of divorce and remarriage is very difficult and involved. Both sides have their strong points, and their values need to be preserved. There is no easy answer. In all truth and candor this is a situation over which the Church today is truly agonizing.

DISCUSSION QUESTIONS

1. Should divorce and remarriage be allowed by the Roman Catholic Church? Why?
2. Complete the statement: "A good preparation for marriage is. . . ."
3. Who should be able to decide if a marriage is dead, never was, or still has hope?
4. A religious marriage (wedding) ceremony is more meaningful than a civil marriage (wedding) ceremony.
5. When do you believe that marriage is consummated?
6. What is the role of the Catholic community in the preparation for marriage? After the marriage?
7. Can only committed partners be good parents?
8. Is preparing for a wedding the same thing as preparing for a marriage?

READINGS

Chicago Studies, "Ministering to Marriage," Vol 18, No. 3 (Fall 1979)

Durkin, Mary and James Hitchcock. *Catholic Perspectives: Divorce.* Thomas More, 1979.

Kelleher, Stephen. *Divorce and Remarriage.* Doubleday, 1973.

Kennedy, Eugene. *What a Modern Catholic Believes About Marriage.* Thomas More, 1972.

Schillebeeckx, Edward. *Marriage: Human Reality and Saving Mystery.* Sheed and Ward, 1965.

Tierney, Terence. *Annulment.* Alba, 1978.

Wrenn, Lawrence. *Divorce and Remarriage.* Newman, 1973.

Young, James. *Growing Through Divorce.* Paulist, 1979.

15 SEXUALITY

Pre-Marital Sexuality

Scripture. Scripture has a healthy and open attitude toward sexuality. At the same time it is challenging, as when the New Testament declares: "Blessed are the pure in heart." "If your eye scandalizes you, tear it out and cast it away." "If a man lusts after a woman in his heart, he has already committed adultery with her." "There is no place for fornicators in the kingdom of God." "Love God with your whole being and your neighbor as yourself." The Gospel tells us to love as Christ loved. The basic Gospel appeal to the fullness of human love, to the total commitment of individuals, to the mystery of married love as witnessing the love of Christ for the Church, says something about the high ideal of what human love is all about. Physical love is but a part of this total human love.

History. Western culture and Christianity have often had a rather negative attitude toward sexuality. This Manichaean tendency of negating the goodness of the physical has a long history and has made various appearances in Christianity. Today, however, we are achieving deeper insights into what a human being is all about, and we are coming to a fuller and better understanding of human sexuality. The Church's traditional position (e.g., its proscription of intercourse outside marriage) is still being upheld, but for much deeper reasons.

Understanding Sexuality. We need a healthy, wholesome

118

attitude toward sex. We need to understand it and to accept it. Sex is an essential, constitutive part of the entire person. All acts of sex involve the entire person and will affect the entire person. Every form of erotic and sexual love that does not have the backing of the total person cannot be regarded as genuine love. Sex needs to be integrated into the whole person—a long, slow process. Christian love demands that we be responsible for all that we do, and that we accept all the obligations that total giving demands.

Sex: The Expression or Language of Love. We human beings are a body/soul composite; we act as a whole. A gesture expresses the total person. We communicate through words, signs, and actions. These words, signs, and actions are expressive of a reality, whether they involve a handshake, a flag, a ring, or a dollar bill. If they do not express reality they are counterfeit. The entire demonstration of sex, in all its wonder, involves both mutual love expressed in self-giving and the acceptance of the resulting responsibilities. Counterfeit love and prostitution divorce sex from its complete meaning.

A kiss, an embrace, and intercourse all have sexual implications. Each has its own built-in meaning. Sex is nothing more than the incarnation of an antecedent love relationship. There are kisses, and there are kisses! A father does not kiss his daughter in the same way that her fiancé does.

Intercourse, the highest form of bodily union, is and should be the expression of the highest form of personal union possible to a human being. It expresses the total and irrevocable giving of self to self with the complete acceptance of all the responsibilities that might be involved. Certain acts (intimate hand caresses of the breasts and genitals) are a direct preliminary to, and stimulus of, intercourse and are to be judged accordingly. If an act is performed which is a sign of this complete self-giving without a complete self-giving having taken place, then it is either selfish pleasure, a crutch, a counterfeit act of love, or prostitution. I must be honest and sincere.

I can express only what I am truly capable of expressing. I can use only the language of love that demonstrates the kind of love that I am *now* capable of giving.

Intercourse: Total and Irrevocable Self-Giving. Sexual intercourse is an expression of a deep, intimate love relationship which demands permanence, fidelity and fertility. It is an expression of a committed life together; it demands an on-going spirit of being alive and of concern about loving each other; it is a state of life that is fruitful in ever so many ways (one of which may be children). All of this equals marriage.

Marriage is not a piece of paper. A marriage license has value only if the commitment has taken place. It is this underlying reality—the commitment—that is important. Since marriage is a basic element of society, society does step in to regulate it so that marriage itself is not abused, and so that individuals are protected against the manipulation of others, and, at times, against themselves. True and authentic unions are based upon a love which is responsible to God, to one's beloved, to society, and to oneself. Societal regulations (marriage licenses) challenge one to see if this is the case for this projected marriage.

In order to see if intercourse is truly the proper expression for any relationship, the following questions might be asked.

- In its totality, intercourse involves the possibility of a child, and a child demands a permanent family situation. If a child did develop in our relationship, would we have to change our current situation in any substantial way? It is understood that a child would always mean some change in even a married couple's life-style.
- Can I use this expression of love (non-contraceptive intercourse) as a regular demonstration of love? I may choose not to use it (and many married couples are so

inclined), but the important question is: "Can I use it as a regular expression of love for this person?"

- If my partner were hurt or were incapacitated for life, would I remain faithful? Would I assume complete responsibility for this person, including personal care and total financial support, until death do us part?

In considering expressions of love, it is most important to consider what is a person's normal expression of love. There are times when our expressions can be more ardent than at other times. There are occasions when we can "skid on the ice." We need to know what is and what should be our normal expression of love at this stage of our relationship with this other person. The Church in its wisdom says that intercourse is not the normal expression of love between unmarried, un-committed people.

Birth Control

The question of birth control needs to be understood in the light of the Christian/Western culture understanding of sexuality over the ages. From the very earliest centuries this understanding was a rather negative one. Sex seen only in terms of babies and pleasure was to be tolerated, but hardly enjoyed. Anyone deliberately ruling out babies was seen as a lustful creature.

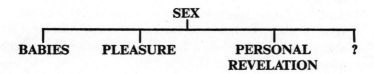

The population explosion has taken place only in the past two centuries. There was no problem before this. Man does have a role to play in populating the world, but it is a human one. He is to act as a human being, and not just as a biological animal, in all aspects of helping, controlling, and ruling nature, both in reproducing himself and in the proper use of the goods of this world.

Marriage has both the procreative aspect (there is no other human way to have children) and a relational or unitive aspect (the personal union between two people). Both must be kept in mind. Love reveres the mystery of sexuality in all of its creativity. The true meaning and purpose of sex is the key to understanding and solving this entire question.

History of Church's Teaching. In 1930 the Anglican Church approved the use of contraceptives on the part of Christians. Late in the same year, Pius XI's encyclical on *Christian Marriage* condemned contraceptive intercourse. The rhythm method was gradually presented as an acceptable approach to the problem. Rhythm itself was a rather crude affair at first, but has since been refined and does present itself as a most acceptable approach for *some* people. The experience of Catholic couples in recent decades has stimulated much research into this question. The Church's traditional stand was challenged by a number of bishops at Vatican II. The question was not thoroughly discussed at the Council; instead Pope John appointed a commission to study the matter. After his death, Pope Paul retained it. This commission, composed of lay and priestly members of the Church, in its majority report recommended a change in the Church's traditional position. The minority report recommended the traditional position.

In 1968 Pope Paul issued his encyclical *Humanae Vitae* in which he upheld the traditional condemnation of contraceptive intercourse. However, he expressly mentioned that this encyclical was not the final word. He urged all competent members of the Church to continue to share their insights and to do more work on the problem in order to come up with a fuller answer. The teaching Church and the pastoral Church are both agonizing over this question. Pastoral statements issued by conferences of bishops from different countries shed fuller light on the question. (Cf. *Catholic Mind* in its issues in 1968 and 1969.) Pope John Paul II has reaffirmed the Church's traditional position.

The Situation Today. There is a universal agreement on responsible parenthood. Only the parents can make the decision about having a child (or another child). They should have only as many children as they can take care of in a proper manner. They need to consider themselves, the existing family, their personal situations, and the demands of the community when making their decision.

Is parenting for everyone? This question is being raised today, and is a difficult one to answer. How do we know we shall not be good parents—especially before we are married and have children? Does this indicate a psychological problem? The fact that there is so much child abuse seems to say that some people make terrible parents. If it is true that parenting is not for us, can we still get married?

The official Church position is still against contraceptive intercourse, but there has been much dissent on the part of bishops, theologians, and parish priests, as well as married couples. It is difficult to say that there is universal acceptance of this teaching. It is true to say, we repeat, that the teaching Church and the pastoral Church are agonizing over this. Basically the argument is over the means used to attain the end, when the end of not having a child now is the responsible decision that has been made. Rhythm is the ideal response, but not all are capable of the ideal response. Sex has a deeper meaning than just babies and pleasure. It is possible that abstinence would not be the answer for this couple at this time. The deep experience of sex might be more important. How should this conflict in values be solved?

Sexuality is multi-faceted. It is biological, sociological, psychological, and spiritual. The teaching Church does have an obligation to teach, to share its insights, and to help all members of the community to see clearly the various values that are involved and that must be considered in answering the question. The married couple, having heard the Church and listening to the voice of God speaking in their own hearts, make the decision. This decision should encompass the following:

- The totality of the person: Every aspect of one's nature (physical, social, moral, religious, psychological, cultural, etc.), one's dignity as a human being, one's call to love God, neighbor and self—all these must be considered.
- The demanding and challenging character of Christian love: It does not allow us to take the easy way out. It often does demand sacrifice of us: "Take up your cross and follow me." "Greater love than this no man has: that he give up his life for his brother."
- An open and searching mind: We must be open to the truth wherever it is found. We must be open to a better decision that can be made tomorrow with changing conditions or newer insights. We must be ready to admit, in the light of tomorrow's new circumstances, that this decision made today is not the best one.
- In this way we make the best possible Christian response that can be made at this moment with a willingness to change tomorrow if newer insights demand it.

Abortion

Abortion, or the deliberate ejection of a non-viable fetus (embryo) from the womb, has always been condemned by the Catholic Church. The Church, though, has not always imposed excommunication on those responsible for it. Today it is looked upon as murder, and all who are involved incur excommunication: they are separated from full communion with the Church and are not allowed to receive the sacraments or to share in the spiritual benefits of the community. Everyone participating in an abortion in any way—the doctor, the patient, anyone urging her or helping her to have an abortion, etc.)—is excommunicated. This excommunication is normally reserved to the bishop, although he can and does delegate to individual priests the power to absolve from this censure. Ignorance of the existence of the excommunication could excuse a person but it is not to be presumed. Today, with the Church's position on abortion so well known, it is difficult to see how any Catholic is unaware of this.

Abortion is not allowed in cases of rape or incest. The woman may receive immediate treatment at a hospital, but not an abortion some weeks later. If and when a baby seems to be a threat to the mother's life, we do not kill either. Both lives are sacred and we must work to save both. At times, however, a pathological condition may exist—for instance a cancerous womb or a tubal pregnancy. In such cases the diseased organ is removed, and with it, at times, a fetus. These are what are called indirect abortions. The direct intention and purpose is to remove the diseased organ; the removal of the fetus is tolerated because there is no way to avoid it. Its removal is not the intention of the operation.

Today the Church takes the position that there is human life from the moment of conception. Over the centuries this has not always been the case. At one time it was thought that the soul of a male baby entered forty days after fertilization, while for a female it was eighty days. There was also the theory that at first there is a "vegetable" soul (i.e., a principle of life that would sustain vegetative activities like taking nourishment, growing), then an "animal" soul, and finally the "rational" or "human" soul. Today there is no absolute proof as to when the soul does enter the body. On the other hand, there is no absolute proof that it does not enter the body at the moment of conception or very shortly thereafter. In cases involving the rights of a third party, we are always required to have certainty before violating their rights, and in this case we are speaking of the rights of the fetus or embryo.

In the United States the courts had always protected the rights of the unborn. They are entitled to share in inheritance, social security benefits, welfare benefits, etc. It was only on January 22, 1973, that the Supreme Court ruled that a woman has the right to an abortion on demand during the early stages of pregnancy, and with the consent of a physician in the middle stages. It still upholds the right of the mother to receive welfare payments for this baby still in her womb, even though it would allow, by another ruling, this same baby to be aborted one week later. It is also interesting to note that a sixteen-year-old girl needs parental permission to have her ears pierced, but not to have an abortion.

Some Pros and Cons. Is the fetus a person? Doctors and scientists see no change from the early moment of conception. It is the same being; it does not change. It is thus clearly human life. There is no later stage when it becomes a person. It is not the same thing as a fingernail. There is a basic difference between a fertilized egg and an unfertilized one. The fertilized egg grows.

Does not the woman have a right over her body? A woman does have this right and can avoid conception. Once she has conceived, however, this fetus is not the same as her body. It is a totally different being and is to be treated accordingly. The fetus is unique, with its own identity and special potential.

A fetus is totally dependent upon the mother. Does the fetus have any rights because it is so dependent? On the other hand, when do children become independent of their parents?

Does the father have any rights?

Abortion on demand during the early stages of pregnancy

demands no justification. The only reason needed is: "I want the abortion."

Population explosion has something to say about birth control, but does this extend to killing others?

Human life comes from God and is sacred. Man has domination over the earth; he does not have dominion over human life. Human life must be inviolate at each and every stage of its development.

Theologian Richard Westley asks the question: "Who should make the decision?" His answer: Only the virtuous person, characterized by vision and self-discipline, can do this. Such a person has a good sense of values, is not blinded by illusions and self-interests, sees the situation clearly and is able to take into consideration the various values and circumstances involved. Such a mature person has good self-control and will-power, is able to carry out decisions that have been made, and is what psychologists might refer to as a well-integrated personality who has it all put together. For a Christian this involves the "spiritual" aspect of life.

Homosexuality

The Christian tradition has always rejected homosexuality as a viable option because it "goes against nature." The current challenge to rethink the question is muddied by the extreme gay activists who do not necessarily represent all homosexuals, as well as by the conservative right wing who claim that God is on their side. Can the Christian tradition, which is to love and to care for all people, accept homosexuality, even though it seems contrary to Christian ideals? How should Christians treat homosexuals?

Homosexuality in Western society has usually been looked upon as an evil to be condemned without mercy. At best it may have been viewed as an aberration, to be tolerated and treated as an illness. Can it be accepted as a viable option for personal growth? To say the least, we do not know enough about homosexuality today. More research is definitely needed. There seems to be some evidence that it is a result of genetic conditioning and is not always an acquired pattern of behavior.

Our research should develop a better attitude toward homosexuality itself, as well as homosexuals individually. In this quest does the Christian tradition demand more of us than would other traditions or cultures? Does sexuality (in its meaning of personal growth and fulfillment) allow for a homosexual expression? Do we have to create a "new" society that will give homosexuality its proper treatment? Like so many other areas, here too it is so much easier to see the problem than it is to develop solutions.

DISCUSSION QUESTIONS

1. Explain why abortion and pre-marital intercourse are examples of being sexually irresponsible.

2. Discuss the impact of the Church's stand against artificial birth control.

3. Is birth control a better alternative than unwanted and abused children?

4. The official Church teaching opposes artificial birth control. It is also taught that a couple should only have as many children as they can possibly care for. Furthermore, intercourse should help the couple grow in love for one another and in union with God. Do these teachings conflict? Should the Church allow birth control? How else can a couple stop from having too many children?

5. What is the proper expression of sexuality for the Christian person who wishes to remain single?

6. O'Neil and Donovan (*Sexuality and Moral Responsi-*

bility) state that when two people are in love but not married, the only real proof that they have real love for each other is to say "no" to sexual intercourse. Do you agree? Why?

7. Explain the statement: "I must love with a celibate love before I can love with a sexual love."

8. Can only the virtuous person make the right decision about abortion, birth control, and pre-marital intercourse?

READINGS

Catholic Mind. September 1968 to April 1969.

Doherty, Dennis, ed. *Dimensions of Human Sexuality.* Doubleday & Co., 1979.

Evoy, John and Maureen O'Keefe. *The Man and the Woman.* Sheed and Ward, 1968.

Kosnik, Anthony, *et al. Human Sexuality.* Paulist, 1977.

McGoey, John. *Dare I Love?* Our Sunday Visitor, 1974.

McNeill, John. *The Church and the Homosexual.* Sheed, Andrews, and McMeel, 1976.

Noonan, John T., Jr. *A Private Choice.* Free Press, 1979.

O'Neil, Robert and Michael Donovan. *Sexuality and Moral Responsibility.* Corpus, 1968.

Oraison, Marc. *The Human Mystery of Sexuality.* Sheed and Ward, 1967.

Paul VI. *Humanae Vitae.* 1968.

Westley, Richard. *What a Modern Catholic Believes About Right to Life.* Thomas More, 1973.

Willke, Dr. and Mrs. J. C. *Handbook on Abortion.* Hiltz, 1972.

16 CHRISTIAN MORALITY

Morality is the way a person acts in order to attain a goal. We are acting in a morally good manner when these actions will lead us on toward our life's goal. We are acting in a morally bad manner when the actions interfere with the successful attaining of our life's goal or even lead us directly away from it. Is there anything special about the way a Christian should act? Does Christ in the New Testament make any special demands upon his followers? He came preaching the kingdom of God. To be a member of this kingdom we have to change our way of life and take upon ourselves new ideals, new attitudes, new principles, and new behavior patterns. Christ came with a new call—the total demands of love and being willing to give up our lives for our neighbor.

If you read the Gospels, the following ingredients stand out: high standards, challenges, conformity to the will of God, concern for others, sincerity, tension, responsibility, universal and uncompromising love. A good summary of what is being asked of Christians could be the Beatitudes. These give us the basic goals, ideals, values, the "be-attitudes" of a follower of Christ. Blessed are the pure of heart, for they shall see God.

Some Emphasis of Recent Decades

The full living of Christ's message has its own history. In the early centuries martyrs were the Christian heroes, followed in subsequent years by monks. In fact for centuries the Christian life reflected that of monks with their detailed regulation of life. In the most recent centuries there has been greater concern for the proper exploitation of one's potential. There is a greater emphasis on our freedom and on personal responsibility. Life is becoming more complex; there are no simple problems. All too often there is constant tension between the demands of conflicting values.

Today there is great concern for the individual, for individual differences, for personal responsibility in an era of extremely complex problems. Yes, I am a member of a group, but I am also a unique individual, with my own personal concerns and demands. This is what personalism is all about. It does not believe that anything goes. Rather, it frees the person for full personal development and then demands that this development take place.

Love is a term that is used so often that it seems to have lost its real meaning. Properly understood, it gives great insight into what Christian living really is. Christ called us to love, not to observe laws. Laws are good; they are the description of how a normal person would act under normal circumstances. They are good guides, especially for the less well educated and the immature. As we grow, however, we are asked to take upon ourselves the responsibility for what we do, and consequently we have to make the decision in many particular cases. Just what should I do? A person who has a good grasp of love and the demands that it makes—that I do all I can for the good of neighbor and the good of the Lord God to whose kingdom I belong—should be well equipped to make good decisions. There is a great need, though, that people understand what love truly is.

Even though we are unique individuals, we as human beings are basically social. We relate to others, we communicate with others, and we grow via our associations with one another. Whatever I do in some way or other influences my neighbor. Whatever I do, I do as a member of this community to which I belong. I either strengthen it or I help to weaken it. Today this social dimension of life is getting more of the attention it deserves.

Finally, Christians are coming to realize more and more that what Christ taught in the New Testament was an ideal ethic. He gave us the ideal toward which we should strive. He did not give us minimum standards to go by. He went all out and told us to be perfect as our heavenly Father is perfect. Each of us has been given certain talents; all of us have to use the talents we have to the fullest. Thus, the Christian position on any moral issue should be that of the ideal response. I may not be able to reach the fullness of the ideal, but I strive to measure up to it insofar as I am able. I never can say I have done enough. I always strive to do more—until I am perfect like my Father in heaven.

Several Catholic "Ethics" or Approaches to Morality

We are all different. What basically is a good ethic for one to follow is not always that good for another. Here are several good ethics that are used by Christians today.

- Authority: Some people are very content to have authority make the basic decisions. I then do as I am told. It is difficult at times to follow these directives, but I do avoid all that trouble of trying to make up my own mind in the midst of conflicting value demands.
- Conscience: To follow your conscience is the traditional teaching of the Church. As I grow as a person, I do have to form my conscience so that I am well aware of what it means to be a Christian and what it takes to make a good decision. I need a good value system and the ability to make good personal decisions. In this growth and development, my community through my

parents, my teachers, and others has had a great role in my formation.

- Love: Morality is a following of Christ. It is entering into a love relationship with God. What was said above about love and about the ideal would apply here. Love forces me to become the best person that I can be so that I have all the more to offer the one I love. Thus I strive toward the ideal; I endeavor to use all my talents to the fullest.

- Tension: In life there are no clear black-and-white textbook situations. In real life the situations are usually complicated; the circumstances of any individual act make the application of the principle a difficult task. There is what might be called a tension between the principles and the circumstances. I must create a marriage between them so that I can maintain the full integrity of both.

A Contemporary Catholic/Christian Ethic

A contemporary ethic that can be accepted and followed by any Catholic or Christian can be described in the following ten points.

1. God is our Creator. God, incarnate as Jesus, is the revelation of what it means to be a human being. God is our Redeemer. God is our fulfillment. We need to know who and what we are, where we came from, where we are going, and how we should get there. A deep investigation of the human person in relation to God gives us great insight into the dignity of all of us and into our purpose in life. God as our Creator has established the game of human living and has set down the basic rules. He made us to be persons who can know who we are, who can discipline and perfect ourselves, and who can direct ourselves personally toward our goal in life.

God as incarnate reveals something about the dignity and

destiny of the human race. There is the divine and human in each of us. Our true destiny involves a very intimate union with the divine. As our Redeemer, God shows his tremendous love for us and reveals that we are worth something. He takes away sin, gives grace, and helps us to realize our goal. He is a personal God, loving and good. He is the only "love" that can truly satisfy the all of me.

2. A Catholic's morality is the free response to God who invites us to enter into a personal love-friendship with him. It is the way we live fully in responding to Christ's invitation to follow him and live a life of love for all (God, neighbor, self). We are called to love God and to be loved by him. This is what it means to follow Christ, to put on Christ.

3. A Catholic morality is a morality of love of God, of neighbor and of self. This is the basic teaching of Scripture where the Old Testament told us to love God above everything and where in the New Testament Christ sums up all commandments in the two of love. This is exemplified by the apostles, by the martyrs, by the missionaries, and by many modern dedicated Christians who give of themselves for the service of all, especially the poor and unwanted. The Trinity is a relationship of love; our relationship with God is love; to attain our goal of love we need to love all. A triangle is not complete without all three (God, neighbor, self).

4. A Catholic morality is a challenging morality. In being ourselves we strive to become our full selves. There is a realization of the highest degree of moral conduct: Be you perfect as your Father is perfect. There is conformity to the will of God. We need to surrender ourselves totally to God in order to be free to become our full selves. We need to be willing to make sacrifices in order to attain union with the one we love. We need to use all our talents. We need to be our full selves, not a carbon copy of someone else.

5. A Catholic is responsible for the full impact of his actions. We do not live and act in a vacuum. We are the same

person all seven days of the week, and we are responsible for what we do and how we affect others. The big question is maturation and breadth of vision. Mature persons have broader vision and deeper insight. They have a keen realization of the profound and far-reaching influence of their conduct both on their own personality and upon their community, present and future. They are responsible (within limits, of course) for acting, and for not acting, for the means used, for the consequences, and for the foreseen effects (in a limited way). This responsibility should not be exaggerated, but neither should it be set aside as of little importance.

6. A mature Catholic must be properly formed; we are not born mature. No one is "absolutely free" but we can work to develop our capacity for freedom and then exercise it. Good decision making involves the following: (a) principles, values, standards which are a part of me; (b) ability to see, to judge, to act, to command self; (c) integration of one's feelings, thoughts, whole self into a whole; (d) awareness of the call of God, of the call of the community to me; (e) prudence, helping me decide here and now what is best.

7. A Catholic operates within the context of a dynamic constellation of values, not a static pyramid. We make our decisions in the light of the entire person which can be summed up in the word IRISH. We are unique *i*ndividuals with our own talents and freedom. We are *r*eligious, called to a deep personal relationship with God. We are *i*ncarnate, a body and a soul, both of which need attention. We are *s*ocial, influencing and being influenced by our community. We are *h*istorical, growing, developing, perfectible persons who exist in a concrete situation. Furthermore, we have to make decisions in the light of the total situation—all circumstances, past, present and future.

8. A Catholic looks to the following for his values and for a clearer understanding of them: Christ, the community of yesterday as well as that of today, the insights of other sci-

ences, cultures, and religions, and personal and prayerful reflection. We get to know Christ both through a careful study of and acquaintance with Scripture and by personal prayer. My faith community has a history, and this shows me how the Christ-event has been lived and taught over the centuries. The total faith community of today (bishops, prophets, parents, friends, etc.) all contribute something to an understanding of living the Jesus experience today. Furthermore, other faith communities, other cultures, and other sciences give me further insights into what it is to be a real human being who believes in God. Deep prayerful reflection should lead to a clearer vision of the values involved and of a deeper understanding of what they entail.

9. A Catholic follows a morality of tension—a marriage of principles and circumstances. There will be conflicts between values, between theoretical principles and concrete circumstances. There is no textbook answer to each question. We need to consider all that is involved, maintain the basic totality of each, and then make the decision which seems best in this situation.

10. A sincere Catholic makes the best possible decision that can be made right now, and at the same time remains open to growth and change tomorrow. We are pilgrims. We are sinners. We are perfectible.

DISCUSSION QUESTIONS

1. What is necessary for a moral Christian to make a free decision?

2. Is morality relative to cultural norms?

3. Which ethic do you feel is for you the best approach to morality?

4. What are your values? Where do they come from?

5. Is Christian morality today too lenient? Too strict?

6. Explain how Jesus, in calling us to be members of his kingdom, demands of us a radical reorienting of our lives.

7. Discuss: Good moral decision making is like good cooking.

READINGS

Curran, Charles. *New Perspectives in Moral Theology*. Fides, 1974.

Gaffney, James. *Newness of Life*. Paulist, 1979.

Lohkamp, Nicholas. *Ten Commandments and the New Morality*. St. Anthony Messenger, 1972.

Maguire, Daniel. *The Moral Choice*. Doubleday & Co., 1979.

McNulty, Frank J. and Edward Wakin. *Should You Ever Feel Guilty?* Paulist, 1978.

Monden, Louis. *Sin, Liberty, and Law*. Sheed and Ward, 1965.

O'Connell, Timothy. *Principles for a Catholic Morality*. Seabury, 1978.

Regan, George M. *New Trends in Moral Theology*. Newman, 1971.

Sloyan, Gerard. *How Do I Know I'm Doing Right?* Pflaum, 1976.

17 THE CALL TO WHOLENESS

Christ called all Christians to follow him and to do as he did—to love, to commit themselves to God, to work at establishing God's kingdom on this earth. We are even to put on the Lord Jesus Christ, as Paul tells us, and, in the words of Christ, to be perfect as our Father in heaven is perfect. Down through the ages Christians have struggled to do so, responding in different ways at different times, but always emphasizing both prayer and works of mercy.

Throughout the centuries Christians have sought to get to know God more intimately and to spend their lives in his presence. Men and women of prayer were always looked upon with great respect and reverence—they were close to the Lord. Their advice and their prayers were sought by others who were unable to spend their entire lives in prayer. This tradition, starting with Christ who spent whole nights in prayer, encompasses the hermits, the monks, religious in the active life, and a whole host of lay men and women who incorporated a full life of prayer into their daily lives. In fact, there can be no good, fruitful apostolic life if it is not backed up by prayer. Good works are nothing more than our prayer life overflowing into our work life, spreading the good news and doing good to our neighbor. All founders of religious societies have insisted that prayer always be given top priority.

A study of the history of the saints in the Catholic Church reveals this call to wholeness. To be whole we need to have our act together. We need to know both who we are and how we are to live as God-related beings. We need to discipline ourselves so that we have all the parts together and are able to use all our talents and capabilities to go out and act as Christians. This is what the saints did, and some of them were blessed with a most remarkable experience of God. We can find these mystics all through the Church's history—St. Augustine, St. Bernard, St. Mechtilde, St. Catherine of Siena, St. Teresa of Avila, St. John of the Cross—and they still abound today in people like Edel Quinn, Charles DeFoucauld, and Maximilian Kolbe.

Religious Orders

Institutions have always been an excellent means both for facilitating one's growth in a certain way of living and for assuring the permanence of a good idea. One such institution is religious life where the various religious orders have both strengthened the prayer life of the Church (Trappists, Carmelites, Benedictines, Poor Clares, etc.) and enabled many good works to flourish (Dominicans, Franciscans, Jesuits, Christian Brothers, Paulists, Marianists, Mercy Sisters, Ursulines, etc.).

In this quest for wholeness, though, we must always remember that the Church is a Church of sinners, a Church of pilgrims on their way toward the Christian ideal of love and service. All too often the pilgrims and the pilgrim Church failed to measure up to what was being asked of them; they needed reminders as to what being a Christian was all about. All through the history of the Church and under the guidance of the Holy Spirit, "prophets" and movements of one kind or another rose up in the community to speak their piece and to point out the way to living the Christian message now. In the very early centuries there were the hermits and the monks. There were the poverty movements of the Middle Ages, ending up with the founding of the mendicant orders—the Dominicans and Franciscans. Hus and Savonorola were reformers who preceded the Protestant Reformation of the sixteenth century. The great number of religious societies that have been founded in recent centuries testify to mankind's quest to follow Christ more perfectly. Vatican II was called to work a kind of "reform" in the Church of the twentieth century.

The Spirit in the Church

The Holy Spirit is alive and well today. More and more people are realizing that the Bible and prayer are the two prime sources for getting to know Christ, and we need to know him before we can follow him. Personal Bible study, alone and in study groups, leads to a deeper grasp of the message of Christianity and to a greater life of personal prayer. This is showing up in various age groups in the Church and is very prominent today among college students and young adults. Many feel that we are entering a decade of spirituality with new trends, new thrusts, and new emphases.

In addition, the Spirit has raised up various groups of movements that are helping Christians to follow Christ more completely. To name just a few, there are the Charismatics, Marriage Encounter, Cursillo, TEC (Teens Encounter Christ) and Search Retreats. Most of these movements are characterized by a strong lay involvement, with much of the work being done by lay men and women. The sessions of a Marriage Encounter or a TEC retreat are highly structured, building up to a crescendo and strongly supported by music, posters, and (for the retreats) letters from friends and relatives. All the movements demand a personal involvement on the part of the participants and provide for future reinforcement and carry-over by special renewals. The end result is usually a strong revitalization of one's life.

It is good to keep in mind, however, that not every group that comes along is the work of the Holy Spirit. The works of the Spirit do need to be discerned. By their fruits you will know them, the Gospels tell us. It is not possible to list criteria that would necessarily apply to each and every movement, but the following three points can be extremely helpful in judging the presence of the Spirit. First, the basic thrust of the movement, its basic teachings and goals, should be faithful to the essential core of the Christian tradition. Second, the movement definitely should lead a person to a closer relationship with God and a resulting feeling of peace with oneself. Lastly, any authentic movement is characterized by humility. The members are not proud, convinced that theirs is the only way. They are deeply aware of the goodness of God and how he has come to them. They appreciate this and would like to share it with others insofar as this is possible. Not every movement is for everybody.

Here follow a few comments about several of these movements of today that appeal to various age groups.

The Cursillo (or "short course in Christianity") began in Spain in 1949 and spread to the United States via the Spanish southwest. It exists today in various parts of the country, especially on both coasts and in the midwest (Ohio, Illinois, and Michigan). Its basic purpose is to enable the participants to come to a new sense of what living Christianity is all about— a dynamic and loving faith. The Cursillo itself is a four-day program, beginning on Thursday evening and ending on Sunday evening. During the course of that time, every effort is made to give the participants a strong feeling for community and to expose them to the basic truths of Christianity as seen today. Priests give some of the talks and lay people give others.

The latter, especially, in their talks show how faith is lived today. To some, it is a highly emotional experience. The solid ones who make it come out as alive and dedicated Christians. They continue to meet together on a regular basis. These meetings or "ultreyas" are a time of sharing, listening to a witness talk or a talk by a priest, praying together, etc.

The Marriage Encounter also originated in Spain and spread to the United States in the early 1960's. It is another weekend movement that is constructed to help couples learn a new way of communicating with each other. As a result they become much more deeply in love than ever before. One of the exercises, basic to the program, is for the husband and wife, separately in their own notebooks, to answer certain questions. After this they exchange notebooks. This leads to a long discussion and to communication on a deeper level than most of them had ever experienced. Some of the questions to be answered are: Why did I come here to this weekend? What are my good/bad points? Why do I want to go on living? What are the feelings I find most attractive in you? In me? In us? What are three occasions in which I felt very close to my spouse? Describe in detail your feelings on these occasions. As for the formal structure (talks, music, posters, etc.) married couples form a team with a priest, and together they make the weekend go.

TEC, Search Retreats: For the young adult (high school and college age) there are a variety of retreat programs that have proven extremely successful. Like all other movements, these retreats are not for everybody. They are successful because the individuals who make them want to be there and the team responsible for directing the program is composed of dedicated individuals (a priest and a number of really alive young adults). Every effort is exerted to make the weekend a felt experience and not just a listened-to experience. The emotional level can run high, but with solid input all along the line, the overall effect is good and lasting.

Charismatics: The Pentecostal movement has existed within the Christian community for many years. Formerly, though, it was concentrated in the Protestant Pentecostal Churches. This fact leads, at times, to a misunderstanding of what the movement today is all about. It has spread throughout all Christian Churches and has dedicated members from all walks of life, including bishops.

The name "charismatic" is given to this movement because of the various gifts (or charisms) of the Spirit that are present within the group. Individuals have a strong sense of the presence of the Spirit and feel guided by the Spirit in their daily lives. Many of them possess the gift of tongues; a certain few have the gift of healing. The really dedicated ones are passionate lovers; they have experienced the healing love of God in their lives and respond to this with a great love of their own.

The groups that meet may be all of one Christian denomination, or they may contain individuals from various Christian faith communities. Their weekly prayer meetings contain readings from Scripture, group singing, shared prayer, etc. They are real celebrations of worship for all those committed to the movement.

Like all movements, this one, too, has its range of participants from the far right (with a spirit of elitism and biblical fundamentalism) to the far left (with an ultra-liberal, un-structured group of people). Real charismatics are extremely dedicated people who have a strong faith in God, a deep spirit of prayer, a love for Scripture, great devotion to Christ and his mother, and a strong desire to serve their fellow human beings. They are aware Christians with a strong religious consciousness and a solid sense of Christian values.

There are other movements in addition to the above. To learn more about any one of them, it is important to get to know the people themselves and, if possible, to participate openly in their programs. Reading about them is not the same as getting to know them personally.

DISCUSSION QUESTIONS

1. What pictures come to your mind when you hear the word "charismatic"?

2. Discuss how Marriage Encounter is a great way of helping couples communicate with each other and reach a deeper understanding and love for each other.

3. Are retreats actually helpful for the teenager in his experience with God and friends, or do they just give a person a temporary "high"?

4. Should the Church recognize all spiritual movements that arise in today's society?

5. Does a person have the right to criticize a movement, no matter how radical, without seeing and experiencing what it has to offer?

6. Discuss this statement: The reason that many spiritual movements are aimed at youth is because they are naive and vulnerable.

7. Are we all called to wholeness, to be saints?

8. To know and follow Christ is it necessary to be personally acquainted with the Bible, especially the New Testament?

READINGS

Demarest, Don and Marilyn and Jerry Sexton. *Marriage Encounter.* Carillon Books, 1977.

Fox, Matthew. *On Becoming a Musical, Mystical Bear.* Harper & Row, 1972.

McDonnell, Kilian. *The Holy Spirit and Power: The Catholic Charismatic Renewal.* Doubleday, 1975.

O'Brien, Elmer. *Varieties of Mystic Experiences.* Mentor-Omega Books, 1965.

O'Connor, E. *The Pentecostal Movement.* Ave Maria, 1971.

18 DEATH AND AFTERLIFE

Christians hold that life is sacred; it is something we have in trust from God. We are the stewards; he has dominion. We have the obligation of taking care of life for as long as it is in our hands. The ordinary means that we use to keep ourselves in good physical working order would include good health habits, taking necessary medicines that are easily obtainable, minor operations, and the like. Extraordinary means usually refer to items that involve excessive pain, expense, or other inconvenience without any reasonable or corresponding hope of recovery or benefit. Such would be kidney machines, heart transplants, or an ocean voyage as a cure. Under normal circumstances no one is obliged to use extraordinary means to preserve his life unless there are proportionately serious reasons for it.

Sacrament of the Sick

In the Catholic order of things, the sacrament of the sick brings out the care and respect that the Church has for life. It is to be noted that this sacrament does not work "magical cures." In times of sickness, though, some doctors testify that those who have strong faith and who are at peace with themselves and with God have a higher recovery rate. The sacrament strengthens the sick person's faith, makes him more at peace, and encourages him in his quest for continued existence.

The rite of the sacrament provides for its reception without the sacraments of reconciliation and the Eucharist, though most frequently on a sick call all three sacraments are fused into one beautiful liturgy. There is a greeting, blessing and special prayers when the priest arrives. This is followed by readings from Scripture, a penitential ritual if the sacrament of reconciliation is not being received, special prayers and then the anointing of the forehead and hands. This is followed by special prayers, the reception of the Eucharist and a final blessing. The prayer at anointing goes as follows: "Through this holy anointing may the Lord in his love and mercy help you with the grace of the Holy Spirit. Amen. May the Lord who frees you from sin save you and raise you up. Amen."

Immortality and Afterlife

There is life after death. All human beings live on somewhere, somehow. We know very little about what life after death is like. Scripture tells us that the eye has not seen what is in store for us in heaven. "In my Father's house there are many mansions." Christ's parables indicate that there is peace, joy, and fulfillment there. There is life there, but it is more properly referred to as the continuation of our present life. These are not two lives but different aspects of one life. What we do here helps to determine what happens there.

All of us are quite familiar with death-resurrection experiences. We die to adolescence to become a young adult, to high school to become a college student, to the single life to get married. This is the theme that is emphasized very much in the new funeral rite in the Catholic liturgy.

Elisabeth Kübler-Ross, from her work with the dying, is absolutely convinced that there is life after death. She says she can prove it from her own experiences with dying people.

Death

Today a more positive attitude is taken toward death. This is an important moment in one's life, but not the only one. What we do with other moments in our lives helps us to determine how we die, and what happens next. The emphasis today on the death-resurrection theme running through our lives, as we die to one thing in order to rise to another, helps develop a positive approach. It is faith that gives us this true picture of death as the gateway to our risen life with the Lord Jesus. There is not much we can know through reason and limited human experiences.

One of the bigger questions related to death is just when it occurs. When the heart stops beating? When breathing stops? When brain waves cease? When the capability of human activity (and not just vegetative activity) ceases? This is an important issue and has some bearing on a number of medical questions. When can you presume a person to be dead so that an organ (kidney, heart) can be transplanted? The determination of the time of death is not primarily a religious question, but it is a legal, medical, and ethical one.

Dying with Dignity

Dying with dignity is allowing nature to take its course and not keeping a person alive by the use of machines. The Catholic position will allow this kind of dying with dignity under certain conditions. Normally irreparable damage must have been done to the human person so that there is no hope for full human recovery, and even if the person recovers enough to cease reliance on machines to stay alive, he would live as a vegetable, not as what we consider a human being. In such cases it is permissible to allow the person to die.

This is not the same as active euthanasia or mercy killing.

The latter takes positive steps to help death come such as poison, drugs, and air bubbles in the blood stream. Euthanasia is never approved by the Catholic Church and seems to be against the very concept of medicine which is a healing profession.

Some authors today advocate the practice of choosing to die, in which an individual, because of very special circumstances, clearly decides for death and the taking of the means to secure it. However this is not dying with dignity. Proponents say that it is not a suicide, but it is not approved as a viable option by the Catholic Church which maintains that it is contrary to the sacred trust in which we hold human life.

In all these questions, there are three main points which keep recurring. One is the hope of recovery. The greater the hope for recovery so that I can function as a human being, even though I might be physically impaired, the more I should strive to maintain life and even take extraordinary means to do so. A second point is my possible contributions to society. The greater the positive contributions I can make to society's well-being, the more reason I have to remain alive, and others should do all they can to help. At times this might even mean a transplant. Lastly, our own basic values, our respect for human life and all that is related to it will have a lot to say about our wanting to stay alive and to take the means requisite for this end.

While alive, can I make a will directing what is to be done if I am ever reduced to a vegetative state? Some states have passed laws which permit this. Other states are considering doing so. The Catholic Church has been in opposition to such legislation. It is not opposed to an individual making such a will, but it does not think that legislation is necessary. I do not need an act of a legislature to give me the right to determine whether I want to be kept alive on machines. I already have this right.

Funeral Rites

In recent decades the Catholic funeral liturgy has changed greatly. Formerly it was a very somber affair emphasizing death. It spoke of resting in peace, but was always aware of sin. Today its theme stresses living forever with Christ. White vestments, a sign of joy in the risen life, are used. The paschal candle is stationed next to the coffin which is covered with a large white pall reminiscent of the new white garment received at baptism. This sprinkling with water recalls our baptism, and the incensation honors the body which was the temple of the Holy Spirit. The entire liturgy from the greeting at the door until the final rite of commendation to the Lord at the end is one of confident hope that we who are baptized in Christ will also share personally in the joys of the resurrection. In all truth, we are going "home."

Limbo

Back in the Middle Ages, theologians who considered the necessity of baptism for salvation were faced with the problem of unbaptized infants. Since the latter could not be placed in hell (no mortal sin), and maybe since they were not in heaven, limbo was "created" by religious thinkers as a possible place for the unbaptized. It is not Catholic Church teaching *de fide*. Today more and more religious thinkers maintain that there is no limbo. Humanity has an innate desire to see and to know God that cannot be satisfied in limbo. Every person, no matter how young, before dying is given a chance to accept or to reject God. God can communicate with souls in ways that we are not aware of. He does not have to wait until a person has reached the legal age of reason. Such a position is much more comforting to a mother who has lost a baby through a miscarriage or had a baby born dead.

Purgatory

If anyone dies without having made full reparation for his failings, purgatory is a place or state of purgation. In Catholic teaching when we sin we have both the guilt and the punishment. When we are reconciled with God the guilt is removed but the punishment may still partially remain. For instance, if I break a window by playing ball carelessly, my parents will forgive me. But because I was careless, I may have to go without a full allowance for a while until the window is paid for. Thus the Catholic Church holds for the existence of purgatory. Scripture seems to imply that it exists (2 Mc 12:39–45; Mt 12:32; 2 Tim 1:18), but the Church's position is based more on tradition than on Scripture. It is difficult to talk about its duration, since it is "in eternity" which is timeless. In our human way of doing things we usually refer to its "duration" because we can understand that better. Some authors present it as taking place in an instant—an encounter with Christ that "burns" away my imperfections, like getting caught in the act by someone you love and respect. Our meeting with Christ could be something like that.

Heaven and Hell

Heaven and hell are ways of describing states of existence after death. We know little about them, but we can conjure up all kinds of comparisons. Today we usually look upon them as states of being, rather than as places. There are degrees of happiness or punishment. Heaven is our goal. It is hard for a real human being to choose to go to hell and then go there, but if we are free human beings the choice is always there.

Christ's teachings give us some insight into going to heaven—or to hell. He compares judgment day to separating the sheep from the goats (those who loved their neighbor and treated them kindly vs. those who did not), or the wheat from the weeds. The road to heaven has a narrow gate. Paul tells us that there is no place there for murderers, fornicators, etc. All are invited, and all who truly love God and their neighbor can expect to join the risen Lord in his kingdom.

Can an all-good and all-loving God allow anyone to go to hell? How could he create a person, knowing that this individual would choose to go to hell? There is a lot about God that we do not know. God does not condemn anyone to hell, any more than a teacher flunks a student. Both permit such things to happen because they must respect the person's freedom. The possibility of hell might even give us a greater insight into the worth of our human actions—how they can merit heaven or hell. They must indeed be worth something.

Reincarnation

Today there is a great interest in the possibility of reincarnation. We find this not only in our interest in the religions of the Far East but also in current novels and movies. We have to admit that there are human experiences and phenomena that are hard to explain. Individuals, under hypnosis, seem to recall previous existences. Is it possible that we Westerners do not know for sure what the Easterners mean by reincarnation? When we study this idea in the religions of the Far East, there does seem to be a lot in common with our traditional teachings on personal growth and development as a full human and religious being, and with the necessity of purgation in order to be united with God in the next life.

The Catholic Church does not teach reincarnation. Some points that do not seem to be adequately covered in such a teaching are these: (1) The uniqueness of the individual—God and *me*. (2) The belief that every person has sufficient means for salvation in one lifetime. (3) The parable of the talents; I do what I am capable of doing; there is no absolute standard of sameness for all. (4) The belief that Christ died for *all*, not just the last reincarnation.

DISCUSSION QUESTIONS

1. Is all mercy killing wrong?
2. Does living a good life help to prepare a person for death?
3. Should our funeral services be a time of celebration rather than a time of mourning?
4. Discuss the importance of keeping life sacred.
5. Discuss how it is through death that we attain our complete maturation in freedom.
6. Is death truly a homecoming?

READINGS

Greeley, Andrew. *Death and Beyond.* Thomas More, 1976.

Hellwig, Monika. *What Are They Saying About Death and Christian Hope?* Paulist, 1978.

Kübler-Ross, Elisabeth. *On Death and Dying.* Macmillan, 1969.

Moody, Raymond. *Life After Life.* Bantam Books, 1975.

Nowell, Robert. *What a Modern Catholic Believes About Death.* Thomas More, 1972.

Shea, John. *What a Modern Catholic Believes About Heaven and Hell.* Thomas More, 1972.

Taylor, Michael, ed. *The Mystery of Suffering and Death.* Alba, 1973.

19 GOD

A philosophy professor once said that the best definition of a human being was the head of a child surrounded by question marks. It has further been stated that an excellent history of the human race could be written just by treating the questions that people over the years have asked. We begin to question as soon as we are able to talk, and we never cease until we die. We are always searching for meaning—the meaning of things at first and then the profound meaning of human existence. Frequently our questions about God are tied in with our search for meaning so that we are able to live a full human life.

God is a mystery. Even when we do say things about him we use "human language" to attempt to explain something which is "wholly other" and therefore not really capable of being adequately grasped by human power and certainly not capable of being expressed in human language. Our "myths" help us to attain reality and give us some insights into "God," but we never exhaust the mystery.

We know more about what God is not than what God is. He is just utterly beyond us. We have inklings, glimmers, but not much more. So much of what we say about him is through analogy. We attribute to him all the good qualities that we see in this life, but we fit them to God in the "most perfect" way possible—always analogically. It is not without reason that the fox in *The Little Prince* says that it with the heart that one sees rightly. I am not sure who is the author of the following, but I share it with you.

God is like Ford; he's got a better idea.

God is like Coke; he's the real thing.

God is like General Electric; he lights your path.

God is like Hallmark Cards; he cared enough to send the very best.

God is like Pepsi; he's got a lot to give.

God is like Standard; you expect more from him and you get it.

God is like Dial; he gives you 'round the clock protection.

God is like Lifebuoy; he gives you a lift.

God is like Sears; he's got everything.

God is like Alka Seltzer; try him, you'll like him.

God is like Bayer Aspirin; he works wonders.

God is like Buick; he's something to believe in.

Existence

Does God exist? Can humans know this? This is not the most important question today when we would much rather ask: "Does God care for me?" Still we can say a few words about it. The so-called classical proofs which we get in philosophy are these.

- Causality. Everything that we are acquainted with needs a cause. As we trace these items to their causes, and then those to their causes, we must finally come to a first being that does not need a cause, but contains within itself its own explanation.
- First mover. Everything in the universe is moved. Everything moved needs a mover. There can be no infinite series. A first unmoved mover must be posited.
- Order in the universe. As we survey the world around

us—the miracle of human birth, the beauty of the flowers, the planetary system, the wonder of the human body, etc.—we find so much order that we cannot say it is the result of chance. We need an intelligent cause.

- Contingency. As we look around us, we find that everything in this universe did not have to be; all are contingent. I am contingent. This book is contingent. This building is contingent. If all things just "might be," then nothing would exist unless there were one necessary being that had to be.

- Perfection. From all the imperfect beings that we are acquainted with in this world, we move, as above, to the one all-perfect being. We creatures, human and material, share in the fullness of his perfection.

To those who are rational thinkers and philosophically bent, these arguments from St. Thomas Aquinas can make a lot of sense. To those who are more concerned with existence than with essence, rational arguments do not say much when we want to experience the deity personally.

Who Is God?

We know very little about who God is. He is one, unique, singular, with no other like him. He possesses some attributes of which we are aware (goodness, perfection, intelligence). God is person. God is love. God reveals himself to us as a Trinity (Father, Son, and Holy Spirit).

Andrew Greeley presents God (the Father, Son and Spirit) under various images as he sees them in the Old Testament and the New Testament. He shows how these images both give us deep insights into who God is and also help us to grasp more fully what Christianity is all about.

J. B. Phillips points out all kinds of false, inadequate, misleading ideas of God and then pursues the question of getting an adequate picture of him. For this to happen God had to reveal himself. He had to make himself fully known to us. This he did ultimately by becoming incarnate in Jesus Christ.

All through history Church leaders and teachers present God to their members. They use different images, symbols, and pictures in their attempt to help their followers get to know God. These images are often colored by their own culture, and they are always inadequate. God is totally other— a mystery. Time does correct these inadequacies insofar as new periods of history bring us fresh insights into God. But these will always be imperfect, and our ideas will be criticized by those who come after us. ERD will always be hard at work on this question.

Some Problems

The more we study God and seek to know him fully, the more problems we run into. If God knows all, he knows what I shall be doing. How can I be truly free? If he is all good and all-powerful, why is there evil in this world? Can there be a hell? There are millions of us, and we are told to pray to God. Can God be everywhere and listen to everyone at the same time? What do we do about the intellectual contradictions such as whether he can make a square circle? Does he have any role in creating the world today? How can there be one God and so many churches that all claim him as their own but do not always treat each other as children of this loving Father? What about the authority that some churches (such as the Roman Catholic) claim?

We must always remember that God is a mystery. The problems are usually on our side of the fence. God is in another "plane," but we can see and operate and understand only in terms of the plane in which we exist. We do not see how the two can be reconciled. That does not mean they cannot be.

God and Me

The most important questions that we ask today concern God and me. Is he interested in me? Does he really care for me? What are his attitudes toward me? The study of the Judaeo-Christian Scriptures and the study of the lives of men and women over the centuries will reveal beyond a doubt that God does care for us. Juan Arias gives an excellent treatment of God caring for us. God loves us. Jesus dying on the cross and Jesus in the Eucharist are tremendous Christian symbols of God's love for us. Truly, he is a good shepherd.

Personal Interest in God

The question is asked: "How do I (each person individually) know there is a God?" Each person can experience God. Some of us believe because of our families. We have grown up among believers and believe through them and with them. Some of us are exposed to the question of God and search him out. We study the experience of the human race. We study the religious literature of mankind. We study our own Christian Scriptures. We study the personal experience that other men and women have had. We pray. We dialogue with God. We experience God—we really have an experience where we "know" that God exists. We have felt him. We have "tested" and learned that the Lord is "sweet," as the Psalmist tells us.

For many this can be an agonizing experience. Our faith-pregnancy can be a most difficult period as we labor to bring forth the adult faith that is within us. The birth process itself can just happen or can be another agonizing experience. At the end there is joy because another "man" or "woman" has been brought into the world. This state of being requires a tremendous openness on our part and a great generosity. When we find the Lord, he shall invite our love. We shall have to respond with a yes or a no. Total personal commitment is as demanding as it is rewarding.

DISCUSSION QUESTIONS

1. Complete the statement: God is ....
2. Is is true that the more you get to know God, the more problems you have with him?
3. Discuss the importance of Jesus in regard to learning more about God.
4. Do we need to experience God before we believe in him?
5. Does God continue to reveal himself to us? How?
6. Is God a personal God?
7. Can humans personally communicate with God?

READINGS

Arias, Juan. *The God I Don't Believe In.* Abbey, 1973.
Greeley, Andrew. *What a Modern Catholic Believes About God.* Thomas More, 1971.
Link, Mark. *Take Off Your Shoes.* Argus, 1972.
Luijpen, Wilhelmus. *What Can You Say About God?* Paulist, 1971.
McBrien, Richard. *In Search of God.* Dimension, 1977.
Phillips, John B. *Your God Is Too Small.* Macmillan, 1969.
Rahner, Karl. *Do You Believe in God?* Paulist, 1969.

20 JESUS CHRIST

Jesus Christ Throughout History

The first Christians witnessed Christ living among them, going about teaching and doing wonderful things. After his death they experienced him as risen, as alive and as present in their midst. During the following centuries, as they reflected on "who he was," the classical approach taken by the councils (Nicaea in 325, Ephesus in 431 and Chalcedon in 451) was developed. Jesus had two natures and one divine personality. He was a real man with a real body, a real soul with a real intellect and a real will. He likewise was divine, the Son of God. Gradually his divinity received primary emphasis. In the Middle Ages there was strong emphasis on Christ as our Redeemer and on his sacrifice for our sins. The nineteenth century expressed an interest in writing a biography of Christ. This led to the question: Did he exist or was he just a myth created by the early Christians? Judged by modern standards the Gospels were not real biographies. At the end of all this search the conclusion was that he did exist. In recent decades there has been a tremendous interest in knowing Jesus as a human being, and in giving thought to the question: What does Jesus mean to me? Finally within the past decade there have been several major works probing the real mystery of who Jesus is as God and man in terms of current thought and insights.

The Jesus Movement

Some years ago there was a very strong Jesus movement thriving in the United States. Many young people, searching for something to give meaning to their lives, latched onto Christ as a way to do this. Unwilling, perhaps, to make the commitment that believing in Jesus demands, many fell by the wayside. Others, dedicated Christians, have maintained their belief in Christ. To them he is very much alive and is a part of their lives. They believe that God loves us and has a plan for our lives, that sin separates us from God, that Jesus Christ died for our sins and he is our only way to God, and that we have to ask Jesus Christ into our lives as our Lord and Savior. Among the charismatic Christians, belief in Christ as our Lord, the one to whom we should commit ourselves, is very strong.

The real believers in Jesus see Christ as our reason for being together as a community, as a Church. It is within the community of faith and love that I encounter the meaning and memory of Jesus. The faith community down through the generations constantly strives to make the Christ-event alive and present. Hence, in this community I can encounter Christ in sacrament, in Scripture, and in its very being.

The Central Figure in Christian Theology

To all Christians, Christ is central. We bear his name. Everything we study about man and man's relationship with God is colored by Jesus. He is the one who enables us to understand a little more what our faith in God is all about.

- He is our Savior, our fulfillment. In becoming man he manifests to us what a human being really is, what our relationship to God ought to be. In his own incarnation (the divine and the human in one person) he gives us an insight into what the grace-nature relationship in a human being can be.

- He is our Redeemer. He freed us from our sins. He gave us the meaning of what life is all about. He taught us how to live this life so that we can reach the goal for which we are created.

- He founded a community, a Church. In a way the Church is a prolongation of Jesus, carrying on his mission today. It is a kind of sacrament in which we can see and meet God.

- Jesus is *the* sacrament of encounter with God. The sacraments in our Christian tradition are faith encounters with Christ and with God. They are sacramental (they occur in word, in sign, in symbol) but they are nonetheless real. In the person of Christ we truly meet God.

- In the summit of our liturgical worship, the Mass, we celebrate the mystery of Christ—the entire mystery of human redemption, from the life and death of Christ, through our own baptism, and on to the union of Christians with the risen Lord in heaven.

- If Christ is God, what does this tell us about the Trinity, about the Father and about the Spirit? Did God reveal himself to us? Does God have a personal relationship with us? Does Christ send the Spirit to us?

- Christ invites us to follow him. "Come, follow me!" What does that have to say about basic Christian morality? What ethical system did he teach, if any?

He Is Risen, Alleluia!

Without the resurrection, Paul tells us (1 Cor 15:13), our faith would be in vain. There is no telling what the story of Christianity would be like if there were no resurrection. The early Christians experienced Christ as risen and as alive and present in their midst. They celebrated this; their approach to following him was one of joy and total giving in love. Over the centuries, however, Christians dwelt more and more on the concepts of sin, redemption from sin, and the passion and death of Christ. Good Friday seemed to get much more attention than Easter Sunday. In recent decades, fortunately, the cycle has taken us back to a deep consideration of Christ as risen. The mystery of the resurrection has been restored to its proper place in Catholic thought and practice and has had its impact on our total Christian witness—in the way we worship, in the way we live, in the way we structure and formulate our beliefs.

The resurrection shows us the fullness of redemption. The total mystery of Christ took our human nature all the way to glory. Too often we look upon redemption as being freed from sins and forget about its positive side of being united to God. In the very being of Christ we see what human nature is to be. Christ's glorified body tells us something entirely different from the battered and bruised body of Good Friday. We are made for "glory"; we should never stop at the cross.

"He is risen" is a cry of celebration, not just an object of belief. "He is risen" moves us in all sorts of ways. Our calling is to live a joyful life and to sit down at the banquet table in heaven. Thus we are to spend this life sprucing ourselves up— in good health, with nice bright eyes, well dressed spiritually. We are somebody! Christian living is more a planting of flowers than an eradication of weeds. This is reflected too in the new rituals of the sacraments: the sacrament of reconciliation,

not penance; eucharistic celebration, not obligation; the sacrament of the sick, not last anointing. Our funeral rites fea-
ture the resurrection and not just death and sorrow. We
worship on Sunday, the day of the resurrection. Christ our
brother is risen, the first-born from the dead. We too are risen
people. We are to live a risen life. We are to live forever and
share in his glory.

Some Questions about Jesus

Does the New Testament call Jesus "God"? The answer
is not a simple "yes." Calling Jesus "God" probably had a liturgical origin and developed largely in the second half of the
first century. There are several clear New Testament references to Jesus as God, but this must be understood in the light
of how the formula "Jesus is God" developed in the Christian
Church in the first century.

How much did Jesus know? Solid study will reveal that
the Gospels portray Christ with some limitations but also as
a person who defied ordinary limitations. In our Christian at-
tempts to understand Christ completely we have always hes-
itated to hold that Jesus had limited knowledge, because such
a position seemed to place a limitation on the divine person.
Scholars are more and more inclined to accept Cyril of Alex-
andria's statement: "We have admired his goodness in that for
love of us he has not refused to descend to such a low position
as to bear all that belongs to our nature, included in which is
ignorance."

Was Jesus virginally conceived? There does not seem to
be any way either to prove or to disprove this scientifically.
The Church, however, from the very beginning has always
taught that he was.

Was there a bodily resurrection? It is evident that the early Christians experienced Christ as risen; this is what the New Testament tells us. After serious research and reflection, Scripture scholars such as Raymond Brown tell us that Christians can and should continue to speak of a bodily resurrection of Jesus. The first Christians did not believe that Jesus' body corrupted in the tomb. Remember, though, that his risen body was not the same as the body we are familiar with.

Furthermore, this resurrection of Jesus is remembered and treasured in Christianity because of what it tells us about what God has done for Jesus and what God will do for us (in our bodily resurrection), since Christ is the "first-born" from the dead.

For fuller treatment of all these questions, consult the works by Raymond Brown listed in the Readings.

DISCUSSION QUESTIONS

1. Do you feel that Christ is as real to you in the Eucharist and the Gospel readings as he was when he was here on earth?

2. If Christ were to become man again right now, how would he come? How would he be received?

3. Is Jesus the reason we come together in a community? How can we encounter Jesus in the community?

4. Could Jesus Christ have been just another prophet such as Mohammed, Buddha, or Brigham Young?

5. Why is it easier for us to relate to Christ than to God the Father or the Holy Spirit?

6. Why is the bodily resurrection of Christ important?

7. What do you personally think of Christ?

8. How are the founders present in the organizations they founded—for instance, Jesus Christ, the signers of the Declaration of Independence, St. Benedict, St. Clare?

READINGS

Brown, Raymond. *Jesus, God and Man.* Bruce Publishing Co., 1967.

Brown, Raymond. *The Virginal Conception and Bodily Resurrection of Jesus.* Paulist, 1973.

Greeley, Andrew. *The Jesus Myth.* Doubleday Co., 1971.

Link, Mark. *He Is the Still Point of the Turning World.* Argus, 1972.

May, William E. *Christ in Contemporary Thought.* Pflaum, 1970.

O'Collins, Gerald. *What Are They Saying About Jesus?* Paulist, 1977.

O'Collins, Gerald. *What Are They Saying About the Resurrection?* Paulist, 1978.

21 MARY

History of Study and Devotion

The New Testament, which is primarily the account of Christ's doings, contains very little about Mary. She is there in the infancy narratives in Matthew and Luke, she occurs in several key passages in John (Cana and Calvary), and she is referred to in several other places. Scholars have written a lot about her, using Old Testament figures and symbols.

A study of art, music, literature and religious devotions down through the ages shows us how much Mary was a part of the basic Christian tradition. The Christian community from the very beginning revered her, and she was the inspiration for a tremendous amount of art and literature. In the late Middle Ages a number of devotions to her sprang up, and in recent centuries she has been the focal point of attention on the part of theologians and devotees. At times some zealous devotees, as they studied her apart from Christ and the Church, gave her too much attention. Her apparitions, especially at Lourdes and at Fatima, again brought her into the limelight. The on-going devotion of dedicated Christians never stopped. In recent decades the theological study of Mary has been put back where it belongs as a part of the basic study of Christ and of the Church. Devotion to her has subsided, but it is still alive. Today there is a very healthy attitude toward the study of Mary and devotion to her. There are some exceptions, including those who want to toss much of the Church's teachings on Mary out the window, and those simple Christians who seem to neglect Christ while multiplying devotions to Mary. In 1973 the bishops of the United States issued a pastoral letter on Mary which gives a good basic account of Catholic teaching about her.

Mary and the Church

Mary has a role to play in the history of salvation. Salvation has come to us in the person of Jesus Christ, and Mary is his mother. The Council of Ephesus (431) declared her to be the Mother of God, and not just of the human nature of Christ. She cooperated in Christ's work. Her consent was required before Christ was conceived in her womb. Her *fiat* ("Be it done unto me according to your word") was a total surrender to God and to God's plan for our salvation. She was there at Cana when Christ began his public ministry and she was there at the end—at Calvary. After the ascension the apostles persevered in prayer with Mary, the Mother of Jesus. She is sometimes called "co-redeemer" to indicate her work in this regard. It is to be kept in mind that in all of this Mary was always subordinate to and dependent upon Christ. She is what she is because of him.

Mary is the mother of the Church and the mother of all mankind. When she conceived Christ at Nazareth, she conceived the "total Christ." All who were to be a part of Christ were conceived then and given birth at Calvary and at baptism. She continues her work as mother down through the ages.

Mary is the archetype both of Church and of Christian. She is the symbol of the way that all human beings should respond to God. Her *fiat* and her living this life of total surrender is the way that the entire Church should receive God and respond to him. It is the way that we should receive God's call—with an open and generous heart, ready to say "yes" with the fullness of our beings. The more we study Mary and become acquainted with her and devoted to her, the more we ourselves will grow as Christians in giving our full response to God. Mary thus gives meaning to what life is all about. Everything about her is understandable in terms of her relationship with God and with this work of salvation.

Some Personal Privileges of Mary

Virginity: It is a Catholic teaching that Mary conceived Christ by the Holy Spirit and not by means of sexual intercourse. Traditional Catholic belief holds that she never had sexual intercourse with her husband Joseph and that she never had any other children. Scripture does refer to the "brothers" of Jesus, but this term can mean relatives and cousins as well as brothers. (Consider the French word "parents" which can mean either parents or relatives.) Elsewhere in the Gospels, some of these "brothers" are referred to as sons of other women. Further, it is a little strange that never, not even after the death of Christ, did one of these brothers come forward to act as a true son and take care of Mary. Scripture scholars agree that the New Testament evidence—either pro or con—is inconclusive. Church tradition will determine what each Christian Church community holds.

Immaculate Conception: It is the teaching· of the Church that Mary was conceived without original sin. She was conceived in the state of friendship with God; she was never in a state of non-friendship. This was solemnly defined in 1854. In her apparition at Lourdes in 1858, she called herself the Immaculate Conception. The bishops of the United States in 1846 named Mary as patroness of the United States under this title of Immaculate Conception.

Assumption: It is the teaching of the Church that Mary

was assumed, body and soul, into heaven. This was formally defined only in 1950, but it had been a firm belief of Christian tradition. Perhaps the definition in 1950 was to give some insight into the real dignity of the human person and the basic purpose of life at a time when the world was concerned with the material aspect of life and was doubtful about our living beyond this life's existence.

Devotion to Mary

Devotion to Mary really began with Christ. God chose to be born of Mary; he made her his Mother. Down through the ages all kinds of devotions to her developed. True, at times these may have gone a little too far, but their basic purpose was good—to honor the Mother of God and to obtain the blessing of God on the devotee. A most solid devotion to Mary is that of filial piety, a reproduction of the state of Christ regarding Mary. It is becoming her son, her daughter, her child, just as Jesus was, and to relate to her as a child to its mother. All true devotees of Mary will admit that the more they honor her and the closer they get to her, the closer they really become to Christ. Mary seems to lead these children of hers close to Christ, and then she steps into the background.

Apparitions of Mary

Many times in past centuries Mary has seemingly appeared to individuals on this earth. Some of these have been sanctioned by the Church; others, lacking sufficient evidence in their favor, have not been recognized. Mary has appeared— usually more than once—to a specific individual with a message and a request. The message most often concerned our being better Christians—doing penance for sins, amending our lives, loving God and neighbor more. The request at times was to have a church built on the spot. Such apparitions, the shrines built, and the miracles wrought serve as a constant reminder to us to keep in mind what Christianity is all about and to live it.

Here we shall mention just three of these apparitions. In 1531 (not long after Cortez discovered Mexico) Mary appeared to a fifty-year-old Indian, Juan Diego. To help him convince the bishop to build a church there in Guadalupe (near Mexico City), during one of her apparitions Mary had Juan pick flowers (which bloomed out of season) and take them to the bishop. When Juan opened his cape to give them to the bishop, the roses fell out but there on his mantle was a picture of Mary. The shrine in Guadalupe is extremely well known throughout Latin America, and Our Lady of Guadalupe is revered by all Hispanic-Americans.

In 1858 at Lourdes in France, Mary appeared to fourteen-year-old Bernadette Soubirous. Mary asked for a church to be built, reminded people that they should do penance for sins, called herself the Immaculate Conception and worked the miracle of the spring. Bernadette dug in the ground and spring waters came forth. They still gush forth, and thousands of people have had miracles worked in their behalf by bathing in these waters.

In 1917 at Fatima, Portugal, Mary appeared to three youngsters—Lucia, age ten, Francisco, age nine, and Jacinta, age seven. Mary referred to herself as Our Lady of the Rosary, asked for penance for sins and amendment of lives, and worked another miracle. Those who were there saw the sun spinning extremely fast, and then it appeared to move back and forth toward the earth.

DISCUSSION QUESTIONS

1. "Mary is the symbol of the way all human beings should respond to God." What does this mean?

2. Is Mary stressed too much in Catholicism? Too little?

3. Mary does not appear much in the Bible, yet she has been studied and much devotion is directed toward her. Why?

4. Mary plays a major role in the salvation of Christians. Explain.

5. Why does coming to know Mary help you get closer to God?

6. Was Mary truly human? Are human weaknesses an essential part of our humanity?

7. Why is "filial piety" called the best devotion to Mary?

READINGS

Brown, Raymond, *et al. Mary in the New Testament.* Fortress, 1978.

Deiss, Lucien. *Daughter of Sion.* Liturgical Press, 1972.

Neubert, Emil. *Jesus, Son of Mary.* Maryhurst Press, 1947.

Paul VI. *Marialis Cultus* (Devotion to the Blessed Virgin Mary), 1974.

Rahner, Karl. *Mary, Mother of the Lord.* Herder and Herder, 1973.

Semmelroth, Otto. *Mary, Archetype of the Church.* Sheed and Ward, 1963.

Schillebeeckx, Edward. *Mary, Mother of Redemption.* Sheed and Ward, 1964.

United States Bishops. *Behold Your Mother,* 1973.

22 THE DEVIL
AND THE SAINTS

What follows here is just a brief overview. Although both topics merit a fuller treatment, this will have to wait another day. More details can be picked up from articles in the *New Catholic Encyclopedia* ("Satan," "Saints," "Canonization of Saints") for which I am indebted here, and from current literature. The "devil" has had his day during the past several years; the "saints" are becoming of greater and greater interest today.

The Devil

Although both the Old and the New Testament frequently refer to the devil, to Satan, and to evil spirits, all such references must be viewed carefully. In the Old Testament the references to devils usually does not mean the same thing that we do today. The devil is presented frequently as an adversary, as the one whose job it is to test man in order to see if he is truly a good person, worthy of the honor and respect he receives. (See the Book of Job.) In the intertestamental period (300 B.C.—100 A.D.) there was a great development in the references to the devil. This was a time of apocalyptic literature under the influence of Persian dualism which believed in two prime principles, one good and one evil. The New Testament contains frequent references to the devil, but careful study will show that the New Testament is above all concerned with the demons as something hostile to man's spiritual good. Christ came and overcame "sin," the "devil," "evil"—all that militated against man's good.

Roman Catholic teaching holds that the devil is real; "he" does exist. The devil or devils (since we really should refer to the evil spirits and not just to one of them) were included in the creation of the angels. Because of their own will, they sinned. God did not create them as evil; God created no evil. The devil does have a certain power over the sinful world, but this is not to be exaggerated. All temptations do not come from the devil. "The devil made me do it" is no real excuse. In no way is the devil to be considered a counterpart of God; he is not on an equal footing with God. Christ came and destroyed the power of the devil (satan, evil spirits) over mankind. The work of redemption and the plenitude of grace involve this giving of "life" to all who accept Christ, as well as all the help they need to conquer sin, evil, and the devil. In baptism, where we pledge our allegiance to Christ, we also make a public renouncement of that which is opposed to the "good" we are to seek—namely, the devil and all his works.

There are legends contained in Christian literature which deal with the fall of the angels, but there are no real facts or doctrine in this regard. However the stories about Michael casting Lucifer out of heaven make for good reading. The "I will not serve" cry of Lucifer is the cry of all those who will not surrender to God and live the good life.

Likewise in our Christian tradition there are references to individuals who made pacts with the devil. Just exactly what these are is not easy to describe. They usually involve selling one's soul to the devil in return for material benefits in this life. They are certainly illustrative of the basic choices offered a Christian—to serve God or to serve the devil.

Can people be possessed by the devil? There are many references to this in Christian history, but we should not be too hasty in reaching this conclusion. Not all references in the past have been to real possessions. Such are rare. The Roman Catholic rite of exorcism, which is the rite of expelling a demon from a possessed person, testifies to the fact that the Church does believe in the possibility of possession. Why certain people are possessed by the devil is not easy to say. These are not necessarily the result of sin on the part of the individual.

The same caution should be observed when dealing with the worship of the devil. There is something that is called satan worship, but it is not always a diabolical worship of "satan" looked upon as the supreme principle of evil and the direct opposite of God.

The Saints

In the New Testament Paul refers to the early Christians as "saints." He considers all those who have accepted the call of Christ to follow him and who are living that full Christian life to be saints because they are committed to God and to his kingdom. Today we use the term to refer to those who we believe are in heaven and whom we honor as having lived the fullness of a life dedicated to God. We recognize that God always takes the initiative in calling us to enter into a love relationship with him, that he allows us to share in his holiness, and that he gives us all we need to live this full life of love.

From the very early centuries martyrs were considered Christian heroes, and their lives and actions were kept in memory. They were given the praise and respect which should be given to those who have lived a life of total dedication to God. They were held up as models to imitate. From the third century on, Christians began to pray to them and to ask these martyrs for the help needed to live the Christian life. This same respect was also paid to other outstanding Christian men and women who, though not martyrs, gave themselves completely to God and to the work of his kingdom, living a life of total surrender to God.

Devotion to the saints grew by leaps and bounds during the Middle Ages and is present throughout the Catholic Church today. The saints are honored because they have lived the Christian life to the fullest, and their help is sought so that we can follow in their footsteps. Asking for their help does not take away from the one mediatorship of Christ. The saints are considered friends of Christ, and we ask them to go with us to Christ for the help we need. We feel more comfortable with these "human" beings as we approach the divinity.

Although all those who die in the friendship of God are considered to be with him in heaven, not all of these are canonized. Canonization is the Church process whereby certain individuals are declared to be in heaven. It is not an easy process today.

In the early centuries the Christian people themselves recognized the goodness of the martyrs and declared them saints. The date and place of their death were both held sacred. The anniversary was entered in the public calendar and their memory celebrated each year. Gradually from the sixth to the tenth century the bishops began to control the process. As more and more individuals were receiving devotion offered to the saints, some official control was needed. The next step would be to centralize this under the Pope. At first papal approval of the cult of a saint was sought in order to give the cult greater prestige and to make the practice more universal. Regular procedures for the declaring of someone as a saint gradually evolved, and today Church law tightly governs the entire process.

Here in brief are the steps to be taken in the process of canonization.

1. *Ordinary Process:* The work begins in the local diocese

where the individual lived, worked and died. The bishop takes steps to see if true fame of the person's sanctity exists, how much, and why. He checks on the solidness of the teachings of the individual, makes certain that no public cult has been offered to the person, and sends a detailed report to Rome.

2. *Introduction of Cause:* The postulator (the person assigned to promote the cause in Rome) prepares what is called a "brief" in which he demonstrates that this person is holy and that there are good reasons to introduce the cause, i.e., begin the process of canonization. The Congregation of Rites examines the request very thoroughly, questioning and seeking out all the necessary information. Upon its favorable report the Pope decrees that the cause may begin.

3. *Apostolic Process:* In a way this is a repetition of what took place in the ordinary process, but now is presided over by Rome and its representatives. The postulator meanwhile prepares for the study of the heroicity of virtues, gathering together all the information he can that will demonstrate that this person lived the virtues of faith, hope, charity, prudence, justice, fortitude and temperance to an heroic degree.

4. *Decree on Validity of Processes:* This is a check to make certain that everything so far has been done properly. If not, the cause would stop here.

5. *Heroic Virtues or Martyrdom:* This is a very long and involved task. The entire life of the person is thoroughly scrutinized, and the testimony of witnesses (if possible) is secured. Serious questions and challenges are raised each step of the way by the promoter of faith, whose task it is to test and to challenge what is being done.

6. *Historical Section:* This is of recent origin. An individual is assigned the task of preparing a solid, historical study of the life and works of the person whose cause is being investigated. This is especially needed when there are no witnesses alive or where no Church documents are available.

7. *Miracles:* There is a serious investigation to see if an

actual miracle was performed and that it occurred through the intercession of the person.

8. *Beatification:* Once miracles have been established, there is a general meeting at which the Pope hears the advice of all the involved Church officials as to whether it is possible to proceed to the beatification of this person. The Pope then issues the decree of beatification and a public ceremony is held. The person can now be called "Blessed" and a limited cult is permitted—limited usually to a town, a diocese, or a religious society.

9. *Canonization:* After further miracles are validated, the cause proceeds to formal canonization.

DISCUSSION QUESTIONS

1. Explain: "The saints are Christian heroes—to be acknowledged and respected as are heroes and exemplars in other areas (inventors, explorers, statesmen, artists, etc.)."

2. What is your idea of a saint? Select some current living figure and describe why you think the person is a saint.

3. Does veneration of the saints take away from the honor due to God, or does it enhance the honor due to God and especially to Christ, the Redeemer of the human race?

4. What is the relationship between evil in the world and the devil?

5. Why has so much attention been given to the devil in modern literature and films?

READINGS

Dorrillet, Jacques, *What Is a Saint?* Hawthorn, 1958.
Langan, Tom. *Harvester of Souls: John Neumann.* Our Sunday Visitor Inc., 1967.

Lewis, Clive S. *The Screwtape Letters.* Macmillan, 1962.
McGinley, Phyllis. *Saint-Watching.* Viking Press, 1969.
Newland, Mary. *The Saints and Our Children.* Kennedy, 1958.
Woods, Richard. *The Devil.* Thomas More, 1973.

23 ECUMENISM

On October 31, 1517, an Augustinian monk named Martin Luther nailed ninety-five propositions for theological debate on the door of the cathedral in Wittenburg, Germany. This traditionally is seen as the beginning of the Protestant Reformation. However, Martin Luther was not the first man to lead a dissenting movement against the Roman Catholic Church. Throughout Church history, various groups of people had disagreed with various Catholic doctrines and had dissented by leaving the Church. Even during the years of the Roman Empire, groups like the Arians, Nestorians, and Gnostics left the established Church. Later, in Medieval Europe, there would be groups like the Albigensians, Lollards, and Hussites.

The first major split in the Catholic Church came in 1054 when the Orthodox Churches of the Eastern Roman Empire denied the authority of the Pope. In doctrine, these churches are basically Catholic. However, there are some major differences between the two churches. Orthodox priests are allowed to marry, although their bishops must be celibate. The Orthodox liturgy is different from the Catholic in that it is much more ritualistic, symbolic and mystical. Today there are several different branches of the Orthodox Church, mostly the result of different churches growing up in different cultures (Greek Orthodox, Russian Orthodox). These churches, which are still separated from Catholicism, are not to be confused with the Eastern rite Catholic churches. The ritual of the East-

ern rite Catholic churches is very similar to that of the Orthodox churches, but the Eastern rite churches have remained in
communion with Rome.

The Protestant Reformation

The next major split in the Catholic unity came during
the sixteenth century. Luther began it, but many educated
men followed him. Within one hundred years, there would be
many different types of Protestantism throughout Europe.

Although there are well over two hundred Protestant denominations in the United States today, they mostly fall into
four distinct categories. The first of these categories is the Lutheran churches. These churches all trace their beginnings to
Martin Luther. They believe in only two sacraments: baptism
and the Lord's Supper. The Bible is seen as the all-important
word of God; therefore personal reading and studying of the
Bible is very important. In some parishes, Lutheran worship
services are still merely preaching services, with no communion, thus serving to emphasize the importance of the word.
Lutherans do not believe in transubstantiation, but they hold
that Christ is present in the Eucharist along with the bread
and wine—a doctrine called consubstantiation. Lutheran clergy are called ministers and they are allowed to marry.

A second Protestant group is the Calvinists or the Reformed churches. These churches all look to John Calvin as
their founder, and in the United States they include the Pres-
byterian and Congregationalist churches. They also accept
only two sacraments and believe that the Bible is the word of
God and the only source of Christian authority. In most Reformed churches, communion is monthly, but more often it is
only quarterly. Calvinists believe that Christ is present spiritually in the Eucharist. Most Reformed churches are not epis-
copal, that is, they have no bishops. Instead the churches are

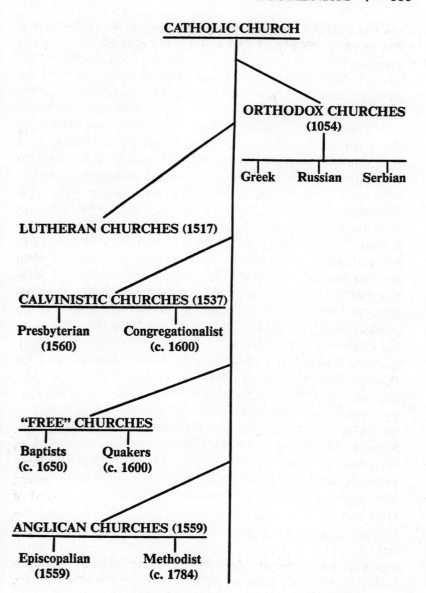

ruled by a general council or assembly, composed of both ministers and lay persons, which meets every four years.

The Anglican churches comprise the third group, established by Henry VIII of England when he broke off relations with the Pope. Henry became the head of the English church. Today, Anglican churches can be found mainly in countries which were once English colonies. The American branch of the Anglican churches is the Episcopalian, which does not accept the English monarch as its head. Instead, it is ruled by bishops who come together in a council periodically. Anglicans are what is termed a liturgical church; they usually have communion weekly. They believe, like the Calvinists, in the spiritual presence of Christ in the Eucharist. Their ministers are called priests (some Anglican churches, like the Episcopalians, ordain women), and their liturgy sometimes is very similar to ours. They respect the same seven sacraments that Roman Catholics do and make use of all of them. However they call baptism and the Eucharist "sacraments" and the other five "sacramental rites." Like all Christians they believe in the importance of the Bible.

The last group of churches can hardly be called a group at all. These are the Free churches. They include groups like the Baptists, Jehovah's Witnesses, and various fundamentalist denominations. Some of them do not believe in sacraments at all. Some believe that because the Bible is the infallible Word of God, everything which the Bible says is literally true (for instance, the creation story). Some do not believe in the Trinity or in the divinity of Christ. Many of these denominations are not involved in the ecumenical movement.

The Ecumenical Movement

For nearly four hundred years after the Reformation, the Catholic and Protestant churches drew further and further apart. There was often a feeling of competition—a race to see who could get the most converts. Then, around 1900, many Protestants realized that this constant bickering among brothers and sisters in Christ was ridiculous. Many of these people were working, fighting and dying in the mission fields together. They learned that as Christians we have much more in common than we have differences. Therefore in 1910 many Protestant Christians came together at Edinburgh, Scotland and formed two organizations, one to deal with worship and one to deal with social and economic problems among Christians throughout the world, especially in the mission countries. In 1949 they came together again to form the World Council of Churches. The majority of Protestant and Orthodox churches in the world now belong to this organization, which meets regularly to discuss matters pertaining to the Christian faith and to social issues.

Because the Catholic Church traditionally held the view that it is the one true Church, it was not initially interested in becoming involved in any ecumenical groups. The first two ecumenical gatherings at Edinburgh and Oberlin, Ohio were not attended by any Catholics. However Vatican II changed that. The *Decree on Ecumenism* admits that there is much Christian truth in the separated churches. Protestants are now looked upon as "separated brethren." Although still not a member of the World Council of Churches, the Catholic Church does send observers to all its meetings.

Today, the ecumenical movement is very noticeable in many communities. It is no longer unusual for various churches, Catholic and Protestant, to come together to form groups which work in improving social conditions. Often, pastors exchange pulpits on Sundays or two or more churches come together to hold inter-faith services. Many Christians have come to the realization that the beliefs of the various denominations are essentially the same. We all worship the same Lord who died and rose for us, we all believe the same Creed, and we share nearly 1,500 years of the same history. Although there are many important differences between Catholics and Protestants, or even between Protestants of different denominations, we now realize that it is better to sit down and discuss these differences than to build walls and ignore one another. The ecumenical movement, while not attempting to eradicate all the differences between the churches (that will probably never happen, and it is even debatable whether it should), is at least trying to help us understand and live what Paul said in his letter to the Galatians: "We are one in Christ Jesus."

DISCUSSION QUESTIONS

1. How important will the spirit of ecumenism be in the future? Will we continue to progress, or is it just a "fad"?

2. What are the basic differences between the Catholic and non-Catholic Christian churches?

3. Should the various churches try to resolve their differences and become one church? Is this possible?

4. Discuss the importance and possibilities of a committee made up of members from various religious groups (Catholic, Protestant, Jewish, Moslem, etc.), working together in the local community. What could such a group achieve?

5. What are the essential beliefs of the Catholic Church (the doctrines that make us "Catholic")? Discuss with non-Catholics their views concerning these beliefs. Are they similar? Different?

READINGS

Bea, Augustin Cardinal. *The Way to Unity After the Council.* Herder & Herder, 1967.
Dillenberger, John and Claude Welch. *Protestant Christianity.* Charles Scribner's Sons, 1954.

Journal of Ecumenical Studies.

Sheerin, John. *A Practical Guide to Ecumenism.* Paulist, 1967.

Swidler, Leonard, ed. *The Eucharist in Ecumenical Dialogue.* Paulist, 1976.

Unterkoefler, Ernest and Andrew Harsanyi, eds. *The Unity We Seek.* Paulist, 1977.

Vatican II, *Decree on Ecumenism.*

Whalen, William. *Separated Brethren.* Bruce, 1966.

24 RELIGIOUS EDUCATION

The Family Is the Key

The family is the key to what has occurred in religious education and what should take place in the future. The family has been the strong central core of the community in most cultures, if not all, and the basic elements of human living were learned there. The same was true in matters of religion. Children learned their basic values in the home. The family setting was where they experienced Christ and a personal faith in God. Formal religious education during Sunday liturgies (those long sermons of yesteryear) and in regular classes was used to supplement this. Since the family had already provided the experience of Christ and had inculcated the values, the schools concentrated on "content." The basic text used in the United States was the Baltimore Catechism which first appeared in 1885 and was slightly revised in 1941. These questions and answers presented the child with a good overview of the basic teachings of the Church.

From the middle 1940's on, changes have been taking place in society and in the family. Some have even referred to it as the breakdown of the family. Society has become much more mobile. Children are being exposed to new and different influences. Family life is different; at times the children are gone more than they are home. The family as a unit spends much less time together. As a result, the family no longer is the only place where the children learn their values. Television, the schools, the peer group, society and its standard of living—all are bombarding the children with different ideas about what is important, what is of value. Children have been coming to CCD (Confraternity of Christian Doctrine) classes without having had an experience of Christ.

During the 1960's CCD classes endeavored to give "experiences." It was felt that students had to experience religion/God/Christ before one could teach them about God. Thus there were skits, discussions, stories, movies, field trips, etc.—almost anything but the formal presentation of the catechism as had been the case. Content seemed to have been tossed out the window, and many parents, students, and teachers were very concerned.

In the 1970's there was a movement to bring content and experience together. But how could this be done? The Christian learner has to experience God and has to make the Christ message a part of himself (bone of my bone, flesh of my flesh, as did the prophet Ezekiel). Remember the two kinds of chocolate bunnies at Easter—the solid ones and the hollow ones? Real Christians are not hollow!

The challenge of today is still the working out of this integration of experience and content. The bishops of the United States emphasized this in *To Teach as Jesus Did* (n. 14, "Message, Community and Service"). Further, we need to determine just what role the family should be playing in religious education. The struggle continues.

The Seven Questions

In an attempt to get a fairly good overall view of religious education today and of the various points that need to be considered, we shall begin by asking the basic questions of who, what, when, where, how, by what means, and why. This is all part of the challenge presented above.

1. *Who* is taught? We all need to become better acquainted with our faith tradition. Children are not the only ones needing further education. Adults—including parents, teachers, clergy, and bishops—also need to keep growing in their understanding of the faith, pressing on toward the goal at which we have not yet arrived.

Who does the teaching? A variety of qualified people are involved. There are parents, teachers or catechists, pastors in a parish, bishops, and theologians. We also need to include publishers and media people who produce books, movies, tapes, etc., for use in religious education. There are a lot of people involved, each with different gifts and responsibilities according to one's call. The Church, recognizing these gifts in some of its members, calls them forth to use and to develop these gifts in service to the community. All must possess the appropriate qualifications.

2. *What* is taught? Basically, it should be the Catholic tradition, a heritage, a way of life (of seeing life and of living life). It is a vision that involves the total person: knowledge, attitudes, values. It combines what was referred to above as experience and content.

3. *When?* Religious faith is taught all through one's life, from the cradle to the grave. There are special times devoted to formal classes (in grade school, high school, college), a variety of CCD programs, adult education classes, parish discussion groups, etc. The general condition of my environment (especially that of the home, the school and the Church at worship) will constantly be teaching something.

4. *Where?* All facets of one's community life should cooperate in teaching about God. Living in a pluralistic society as we do, this is not always done. One facet does not always support another. Hence there is an even greater responsibility to see that religion is taught in our Catholic schools, in our parishes (both in liturgy and in adult education programs), and in our colleges and universities. Very much can be done

in the home, as a regular part of family education and even as a locale for CCD classes.

5. *How* is religion taught? A distinction may be made between teaching in order to catechize one in the faith (in grade school especially, though it comes at other times too) and teaching in order to help persons already catechized to understand their faith better. Normally a teacher is a sincere believer in the faith tradition of this community. The teacher is a seeker after truth wherever it is found, a pilgrim who has not yet reached full possession of the truth, a committed member of this community. When the task is more theologizing than catechizing (e.g., college classes) representatives of other faith traditions can have a lot to offer us. They approach things from different backgrounds and help to throw additional light on the topics under discussion. The role of the believing teacher, though, is also very important. All such teachers must be properly qualified and proceed in an academic manner.

6. *By what means?* There are formal classes, workshops, lectures, retreats, cursillos, marriage encounters, etc. There are all kinds of things to read: books, newspapers, magazines. The Sunday liturgy can be a fruitful source of instruction. One can use the lecture method, discussion groups, movies, field trips, activities, and pageants. In other words, use every means available.

7. *Why?* All education and formation should lead to the calling forth of the individuals' personal commitment to the Catholic faith community so that they will be able to live the Catholic heritage today, pass on an enriched Catholic heritage to the world of tomorrow, and contribute to the mission of the community.

Some Current Developments

Formerly we relied very heavily on the Catholic school to teach children the rudiments of their faith tradition. Dedicated religious, along with the parish priest, were capable of giving basic instruction. Today education is a much more sophisticated process, and there are more and more students not in the Catholic school system. This has necessitated taking a good hard look at what has been going on and taking steps to improve the situation.

Many dioceses are in the process of drawing up standards and criteria for all religion teachers to meet, both CCD teachers as well as those in Catholic grade schools and high schools. The move is to have professionals do the teaching in all religious education programs. This will mean hiring full-time people instead of relying on parish volunteers for CCD programs especially.

There is a wide variety of good texts for the various classes at different levels. In addition there are parish and diocesan resource centers being established so that all kinds of extra things, especially in the audio-visual line, are available for the community.

In some parishes the team ministry approach is being used. All those involved in the mission of the parish—pastor, music director, youth minister, religious education director— work together as a team, rather than as individuals carrying out the decisions made by the one on top.

There is greater and greater emphasis today placed on adult education programs and on continuing education programs for the clergy. We should never stop learning. Parents are being involved more and more in the initial stages of catechizing the children. Frequently parents are the ones who prepare the child for First Communion and first confession.

All this growth and development has not been without problems. There is still the job of selling many parishes on the need for professional teachers of religion and the proper financial support for a total parish religious education program. Then, too, try selling new programs to students who have experienced bad ones!

With the growth of suburbia, the Catholic Church has experienced a decline in its school population, for not all parishes had the resources to invest in a grade school. In addition, many suburban public schools provide an excellent education, and often families are not able to handle the costs involved in sending their children to a Catholic school. Thus, the entire Catholic school system has come under serious investigation. Should we maintain schools? Should we cut back and handle only certain grades? If so, which ones?

Many reports seem to indicate that Catholic families are willing to support Catholic grade schools. They want a school, but it must be a good one, giving quality education, on a par with any public school. Most have found that overall there is more personal attention in a private school and that the religious motivation present there is lacking in a public school. It is always difficult to make comparisons. Some public schools are better than some private schools; some private schools are better than some public schools. This entire matter is a serious question both for the Church community as a whole and for the individual families. Should there be a Catholic school? Are we willing to make the sacrifices this demands? Schools are a most important part of any community.

DISCUSSION QUESTIONS

1. Should all persons of all faiths receive some type of religious education in order that they may more fully understand the religion that they believe in?

2. Is religious education for small children really religious programming? Is this good or bad?

3. Is it true that adults often know less about their faith than their children do? In order to change this, is some type of adult education necessary?

4. What is the role of parents and the entire family in religious education?

5. Do you feel that your own religious education met your needs?

6. In religious education, what do you feel should be taught—knowledge? attitudes? values? What is the importance of each?

7. Discuss some possible ways to better educate adults and children in their faith.

8. Describe a good religious education program.

READINGS

Bishops of the United States. *To Teach as Jesus Did,* 1972; *Basic Teachings for Catholic Religious Education,* 1973; *Sharing the Light of Faith,* 1979.

25 A ROMAN CATHOLIC TODAY—SUMMARY NOTIONS

In this final section we shall present two summaries of what a Roman Catholic is today. Each in its own way summarizes much of what has gone before and seeks to present a picture of what such a person should be like today.

The Catholic Church Today

The Catholic Church today is itself a witness of *evolution,* not revolution, in its growth and development. It endeavors to take the good and the true from wherever it is found. Religion today has become much more personal.

There is a legitimate *pluralism* existing in Roman Catholicism. There are different possible approaches. This does not mean that every approach is all right. Some still are not; sin and error do exist. Unfortunately, too many people automatically identify their "own" thinking with "acceptable" Roman Catholic teaching. This is not always true. We all need to listen to the official teachers in the community.

The exact nature and mission of the Catholic Church vis-à-vis the "kingdom of God" is much discussed today. Kingdom is a broader concept and includes all of creation. The

Catholic Church is a narrower concept and can be seen as *a* (not the only) *leaven* that helps to bring about the realization of the kingdom of God here and now. The way we view this is important and will influence much of our other thinking regarding Catholicism today.

In this age of personalism and individualism, *authority* still has a right and a responsibility to teach (and to prepare itself for good teaching) and to lead. Every sincere Catholic must listen to the voice of the Church's teaching authority. Some people will always need help. Others, while growing, need to be taught correctly. All can benefit from the insights of experienced people. In cases of great complexity, doubt and difficulty, or even "equal option" cases, Church authority has the right and the responsibility to make a decision. The teaching/learning Church does have to face up to some very complex and agonizing problems that do not lend themselves to simple solutions. At times, Church authority is not able to come up with *the* answer. There will always be mysteries in life.

In order to measure up to their responsibilities today, all Catholics have to attain a high degree of personal *maturation*—become a total person, fully educated, integrated, i.e., become virtuous.

It is necessary that Catholics continue their religious education all through their life. *Updating* can be done by the reading of contemporary books and articles, by attending lectures and short-term courses, by participating in discussion groups, and by dialoguing with others who know a bit more than they do.

Membership in a community involves *commitment to the community* and to that for which the community stands—its principles, its faith-teachings, its moral standards. If we cannot accept them, we should acknowledge this and either be a member struggling to measure up to community ideals, or, if necessary, leave the community. There is always room, while remaining a member of the community, for helping the community to grow.

The basic *belief* of a Catholic today is still summed up in the Apostles' Creed. However, the truths may often be explained or presented in different "words."

The *moral code* of a Catholic may be summed up by three ideas: (a) the triangle of love (God, neighbor, self), (b) the ideal rather than the minimal, and (c) a marriage of principles and situations.

The basic *cult* of a Catholic today is a meaningful worship centered in the Eucharist. The core remains the same, although there may be differences in the various external expressions.

A Roman Catholic Today Should Be:

A member of a community. The faith community sets certain parameters (creed, code, cult, organization) which each member is to accept, cooperate with and be committed to. The member can always work for the growth and development of the community, and one should be supportive of one's fellow members. The Church in the past centuries always was a community. The community must exist "outside" the Church before it will be there on the "inside." In these times of mobility, members need to work at supports which are not automatically there. They must give of their time and interest by being a real part of the group. The member must contribute to his neighborhood. This is being ecumenical in the real, broad sense of the term. The Church and world really are *one*. The member is a part of the whole: local, state, national and international. All social issues concern each member and the entire world, the entire human race.

A pregnant pilgrim amid a pregnant people. The people of God have a history which shows that they are always pilgrims and always pregnant with the problems of the times (impact of local culture) and in the process of bringing to birth a "new" Church which again will be pregnant with the "next" edition. This age sees them struggling with the problems of today. The people of God are not always quick to catch on; some are slow learners, but they do learn. Some are too wrapped up in the little things, in the peripheral items. Pilgrims recognize that they are not yet perfect, that they do not have all the answers, and certainly not the final answer. They make mistakes which they recognize, accept, and then work on in order to improve. They are witnesses to evolution, not revolution. There will be a variety of pregnancies. All do not grow up in the same way; God speaks to his people in many ways. The people of God hold to the truth, rather than to "idols" (expressions of truths at one time in history). They are perpetual students of history, of all aspects of our current times, of the meaning of the Christian message today. This is done via a broad range of reading, classes, lectures, and discussions. The pilgrims constantly update themselves.

A leavening member. Since the members of the faith community are also members of the world community, the communities are in reality closely interrelated. Faith community members leaven both. They take the Gospel seriously. They are all the kingdom of God, and if the salt loses its taste, what is to happen? They are the leaven that makes this faith community and this world community what they are. There is need for continued personal growth, for bringing an adult faith to birth.

An idealist. The members believe they are sons and daughters of God, called to a love relationship, which is most intimate and most demanding. Their ideal demands that they seek to be perfect as their heavenly Father is perfect. Thus, their response to him must be total, with all their talents. They follow a morality of tension. This is no TV dinner morality, no "off-the-rack" solution. They must be their own chef and tailor. They must put circumstances and principles together for the best possible Christian response now.

A contributing member. The members must participate actively according to their own time and talents. They are pilgrims, not yet perfect. Both the community and the individual member will be alive insofar as they are "in action." The community is what the members make it to be. The community can demand sacrifices of its members.

A loyal member, willing to speak up. The members listen to the leadership and seek to understand what is meant rather than said. The members are open-minded, not closed or prejudiced in advance. They ask questions. They contribute to the ERD process. If they disagree, they do so responsibly, knowing that at times they must disagree. They do so only in areas of personal competence; otherwise they continue to ask questions of those who are competent. They do so in a responsible manner—quietly (using Gospel correction procedures), with respect for authority and the less informed, as a member of this faith community, pledged to help it grow, seeking the fullness of truth rather than any personal grandeur.

These are some ways of looking at what a Roman Catholic should be today. These characteristics can be applied to all aspects of living: worship life, social life, political life, neighborhood life, job life, education life, etc. All help the faith community realize its role in building up the kingdom of God throughout the universe.

DISCUSSION QUESTIONS

1. Discuss whether the Catholic's role in the community is any different than that of, say, a Methodist or a Lutheran.

2. Is there enough participation in today's Catholic Church?

3. Someone once said that it is easy to be called a Catholic, but difficult to be one. Comment.

4. Write out your own creed or profession of what you truly believe.

5. At this point in your life, do you consider yourself more of a pregnant pilgrim, a leavening member, an idealist, a contributing member or a loyal member of the Church?

6. Draw up your own summary description of what a Roman Catholic today is or ought to be.

READINGS

Magazines/Newspapers/References

The U.S. Catholic
National Catholic Reporter
Diocesan newspaper
America
Commonweal
Catholic Mind
The New Catholic Encyclopedia

Books

Dyer, George, ed. *An American Catechism.* Seabury, 1975.

Greeley, Andrew. *The Great Mysteries.* Seabury, 1976.

Greeley, Andrew. *The New Agenda.* Doubleday, 1973.

Hardon, John. *The Catholic Catechism.* Doubleday, 1975.

Lawler, Ronald, Donald Wuerl, and Thomas Lawler, eds. *The Teaching of Christ.* Our Sunday Visitor, 1976.

Wilhelm, Anthony. *Christ Among Us.* Paulist, 1973.

26 PRAYERS AND PRACTICES

Sign of the Cross

In the name of the Father,
and of the Son,
and of the Holy Spirit.

Amen.

Our Father

Our Father, who art in heaven, hallowed be thy name;
thy kingdom come; thy will be done on earth as it is in heaven.
Give us this day our daily bread; and forgive us our trespasses
as we forgive those who trespass against us; and lead us not
into temptation, but deliver us from evil. Amen.

Hail Mary

Hail, Mary, full of grace. The Lord is with you. Blessed
are you among women, and blessed is the fruit of your womb,
Jesus. Holy Mary, Mother of God, pray for us sinners, now
and at the hour of our death. Amen.

Glory Be

Glory to the Father, and to the Son, and to the Holy Spirit, as it was in the beginning, is now, and will be forever. Amen.

Apostles' Creed

I believe in God, the Father almighty, Creator of heaven and earth; and in Jesus Christ, his only Son, our Lord, who was conceived by the Holy Spirit, born of the virgin Mary, suffered under Pontius Pilate, was crucified, died, and was buried. He descended into hell; the third day he arose again from the dead; he ascended into heaven, sits at the right hand of God, the Father almighty; from thence he shall come to judge the living and the dead. I believe in the Holy Spirit, the holy Catholic Church, the communion of saints, the forgiveness of sins, the resurrection of the body, and life everlasting. Amen.

Act of Oblation

O my God, in union with Jesus, Mary, and Joseph, I offer and consecrate to you my mind, my heart, my body, all that I am, all that I have, and all that I shall do and suffer this day.

Memorare

Remember, O most gracious Virgin Mary, that never was it known that anyone who fled to your protection, implored your help or sought your intercession was left unaided. Inspired with this confidence, I fly to you, O virgin of virgins, my mother. To you I come, before you I stand, sinful and sorrowful. O Mother of the Word Incarnate, despise not my petitions, but in your mercy, hear and answer me. Amen.

Hail, Holy Queen

Hail, holy queen, mother of mercy, our life, our sweetness, and our hope. To you do we cry, poor banished children of Eve; to you do we send up our sighs, mourning and weeping in this valley of tears. Turn then, O most gracious advocate, your eyes of mercy toward us, and after this our exile, show us the blessed fruit of your womb, Jesus. O clement, O loving, O sweet virgin Mary.

Angelus

The angel of the Lord declared unto Mary.
And she conceived of the Holy Spirit. (Hail Mary)

Behold the handmaid of the Lord.
May it be done unto me according to your word. (Hail Mary)

And the Word was made flesh.
And dwelt among us. (Hail Mary)

Pray for us, O holy Mother of God.
That we may be made worthy of the promises of Christ.

Let us pray. O Lord, it was through the message of an angel that we learned of the incarnation of Christ, your son. Pour your grace into our hearts, and by his passion and cross bring us to the glory of his resurrection. Through Christ, our Lord. Amen.

Queen of Heaven

Queen of heaven, rejoice alleluia.

The Son whom you were privileged to bear, alleluia, has risen as he said, alleluia.

Pray to God for us, alleluia. Rejoice and be glad, Virgin Mary, alleluia.

For the Lord has truly risen, alleluia.

Let us pray. O God, it was by the resurrection of your Son, our Lord Jesus Christ, that you brought joy to the world. Grant that through the intercession of the Virgin Mary, his Mother, we may attain the joy of eternal life. Through Christ, our Lord.

Come Holy Spirit

Come, Holy Spirit,
fill the hearts of your faithful,
and kindle in them the fire of your love.
Send forth your Spirit and they shall be created,
and you shall renew the face of the earth.

Let us pray. O God, who taught the hearts of the faithful by the light of your Holy Spirit, grant us in the same Spirit to relish what is right, and evermore to rejoice in his holy comfort. Through Christ our Lord. Amen.

Prayer of St. Francis

Lord, make me an instrument of your peace;
That where there is hatred, I may bring love;
That where there is wrong, I may bring the spirit of
    forgiveness;
That where there is discord, I may bring harmony;
That where there is error, I may bring truth;
That where there is despair, I may bring hope;

That where there are shadows, I may bring your light;
That where there is sadness, I may bring joy.
Lord, grant that I may seek rather to comfort, than to
   be comforted;
To understand, than be to understood;
To love, than to be loved.
For it is by giving that one receives;
It is by self-forgetting that one finds;
It is by forgiving that one is forgiven;
It is by dying that one awakens to eternal life.

An Act of Contrition

My God, I am sorry for my sins with all my heart. In choosing to do wrong and failing to do good, I have sinned against you whom I should love above all things. I firmly intend, with your help, to do penance, to sin no more, and to avoid whatever leads to sin. Our Saviour Jesus Christ suffered and died for us. In his name, my God, have mercy.

Commandments of God

1. You shall honor no other God but me.
2. You shall not misuse the name of the Lord your God.
3. Remember to keep holy the Sabbath day.
4. Honor your father and your mother.
5. You shall not kill.
6. You shall not commit adultery.
7. You shall not steal.
8. You shall not bear false witness against your neighbor.
9. You shall not covet your neighbor's wife.
10. You shall not covet your neighbor's goods.

Commandments of the Church

1. Assist at Mass on Sundays and holy days; avoid unnecessary work on these days.
2. Fast and abstain on the days appointed.
3. Confess your sins at least once a year.
4. Receive Holy Communion during the Easter time.
5. Contribute to the support of the Church.
6. Observe the laws of the Church concerning marriage.

Beatitudes

1. Blessed are the poor in spirit; the reign of God is theirs.
2. Blessed are the sorrowing; they shall be consoled.
3. Blessed are the lowly; they shall inherit the land.
4. Blessed are they who hunger and thirst for holiness; they shall have their fill.
5. Blessed are they who show mercy; mercy shall be theirs.
6. Blessed are the single-hearted; they shall see God.
7. Blessed are the peacemakers; they shall be called sons of God.
8. Blessed are those persecuted for holiness' sake; the reign of God is theirs.

Corporal Works of Mercy

1. To feed the hungry.
2. To give drink to the thirsty.
3. To clothe the naked.
4. To visit the imprisoned.
5. To shelter the homeless.
6. To visit the sick.
7. To bury the dead.

Spiritual Works of Mercy

1. To admonish the sinner.
2. To instruct the ignorant.
3. To counsel the doubtful.
4. To comfort the sorrowful.
5. To bear wrongs patiently.
6. To forgive all injuries.
7. To pray for the living and the dead.

The Rosary

The complete rosary is composed of fifteen decades, but ordinarily only one part (or set of mysteries) is said at a time. The rosary begins with the Apostles' Creed, an Our Father, three Hail Marys and a Glory to the Father. Then follow the five decades in honor of the five joyful (or sorrowful or glorious) mysteries. While reflecting on each mystery an Our Father, ten Hail Marys and one Glory to the Father are said.

Joyful Mysteries:

1. Annunciation
2. Visitation
3. Birth of Jesus
4. Presentation of Jesus in the Temple
5. Finding of Jesus in the Temple

Sorrowful Mysteries:

1. Agony in the Garden
2. Scourging at the Pillar
3. Crowning with Thorns
4. Carrying of the Cross
5. Crucifixion

Glorious Mysteries:

1. Resurrection
2. Ascension
3. Descent of the Holy Spirit
4. Assumption of Mary
5. Coronation of Mary as Queen

Way of the Cross

1. Jesus is condemned to death on the cross.
2. Jesus accepts his cross.
3. Jesus falls the first time.
4. Jesus meets his sorrowful Mother.
5. Simon of Cyrene helps Jesus carry his cross.
6. Veronica wipes the face of Jesus.
7. Jesus falls the second time.
8. Jesus speaks to the women of Jerusalem.
9. Jesus falls the third time.
10. Jesus is stripped of his garments.
11. Jesus is nailed to the cross.
12. Jesus dies on the cross.
13. Jesus is taken down from the cross.
14. Jesus is placed in the tomb.
(15. Jesus rises from the dead.)

Sacrament of Reconciliation

After personal prayer and reflection the penitent enters the reconciliation room (or confessional) and is greeted warmly by the confessor who invites the penitent to trust in God. Then follows an optional reading from Scripture. The penitent then confesses, using whatever formula he is accustomed to. He endeavors to manifest his state of conscience rather than give a grocery list. This often includes a certain amount of dialogue as the confessor and penitent seek to discover what should be done in order for the penitent to grow. There is the imposing of some personal act of penance or satisfaction. The penitent then prays, asking for forgiveness. The confessor pronounces the words of absolution, holding his hands over the penitent (or at least extending his right hand). The words of absolution and the dismissal of the penitent go like this:

God, the Father of mercies, through the death and resurrection of his Son has reconciled the world to himself and sent the Holy Spirit among us for the forgiveness of sins; through the ministry of the Church, may God give you pardon and peace, and I absolve you from your sins in the name of the Father, and of the Son, and of the Holy Spirit. Amen.

Give thanks to the Lord, for he is good. His mercy endures forever.

The Lord has freed you from your sins. Go in peace.

THE MASS

Introduction

Important events often begin with appropriate mood-setting rituals. This is what the introductory rites of the Mass accomplish. The greeting ties us together as a community. The celebrant's opening words set the theme for today's liturgy. The brief penitential rite calls to our mind our own weakness and the loving kindness of our God. The hymn of praise (Sundays and feast days) and the concluding prayer put us into a positive receptive frame of mind for what is to come.

Liturgy of the Word

This part of the Mass is a carry-over from the Jewish temple service and centers on the reading of God's word. There are several selections from the Old and New Testaments (two on weekdays and three on Sundays) featuring a unified theme when possible. The readings are followed either by a silent pause for reflection or by a responsory that is better sung than read. A homily, based on the scriptural readings, concludes this part of the service. On Sundays there is also the profession of faith through the praying of the Nicene Creed.

Liturgy of the Eucharist

This part of the liturgy moves smoothly but unhurriedly through three stages: the preparation of gifts, the eucharistic prayer, and Communion. It is usually begun by the congregation praying together for special intentions recommended to them (Prayer of the Faithful). After this the gifts are prepared on the altar. Frequently there is a procession whereby the congregation presents the basic gifts of bread and wine (and at times the offertory collection) to the celebrant. These are placed on the altar, accompanied by appropriate prayers.

The great eucharistic prayer of thanks begins with a preface or hymn of praise to the Lord which ends with the singing of the Holy, Holy, Holy. The eucharistic prayer proper recalls to our minds the great events whereby we were saved (the life, death and resurrection of Christ) and includes special prayers to and for all members of the Christian community, both living and dead. At its center is the consecration of the bread and wine into the body and blood of Christ. It concludes with the great "Amen" whereby the entire congregation places its seal of approval on what is taking place.

The Communion ritual includes the praying of the Our Father, an exchange of a sign of peace and fellowship (unless this has occurred elsewhere in the Mass), appropriate prayers, and the partaking of the Eucharist under the species of bread, and at times of wine.

Conclusion

After the pause for private reflection after Communion, the Mass concludes with a final prayer, a blessing, and a sending forth to live the message taught and learned both in the liturgy of the word and in the liturgy of the Eucharist. Go in peace to love and serve the Lord.